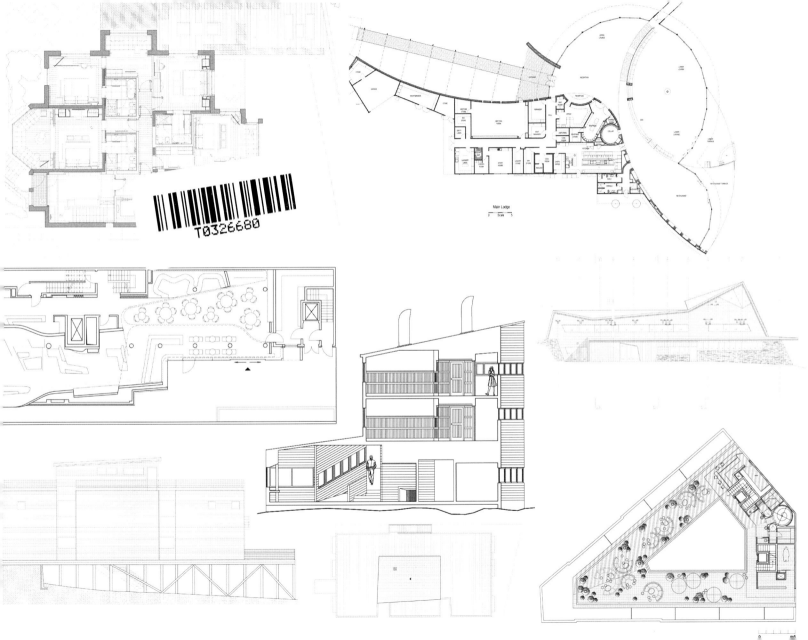

Main Lodge

0    Scale    5

# HOTELPLANS

© 2019 Instituto Monsa de ediciones.

First edition in 2019 by Monsa Publications,
Gravina 43 (08930) Sant Adrià de Besós.
Barcelona (Spain) T +34 93 381 00 50
www.monsa.com monsa@monsa.com

Editor and Project Director Anna Minguet
Art director Eva Minguet
Layout Marc Giménez
(Monsa Publications)
Printing Grafo

Shop online:
www.monsashop.com

Follow us!
Instagram: @monsapublications
Facebook: @monsashop

ISBN: 978-84-17557-09-6
B 23416-2019
November 2019

# HOTELPLANS

monsa

Hotel Plans contains more than 300 floor and elevations plans, as well as constructive details of 35 hotels projects from around the world, selected for being singular and unique hotels, both by their architecture and their interior design, that run away from the typical concept of standard hotel and are conceived for travellers looking for a different and unforgettable place to lodge.

Many of these hotels even offer discotheques, terraces, restaurants or reading rooms... The majority of them are located in major cities, although some are in rural settings.

Hotel Plans contiene más de 300 planos de plantas, secciones, bocetos y alzados, así como detalles constructivos de un total de 35 proyectos de hoteles de todo el mundo, seleccionados por ser singulares y únicos tanto por su arquitectura como por su diseño interior, que huyen del concepto típico de hotel estándar, y están pensados para viajeros que buscan un sitio diferente e inolvidable donde hospedarse.

Muchos cuentan con espacios como discoteca, terraza, restaurante, o sala de lectura... La mayoría de los proyectos presentados están situados en grandes ciudades, aunque también los hay en entornos rurales.

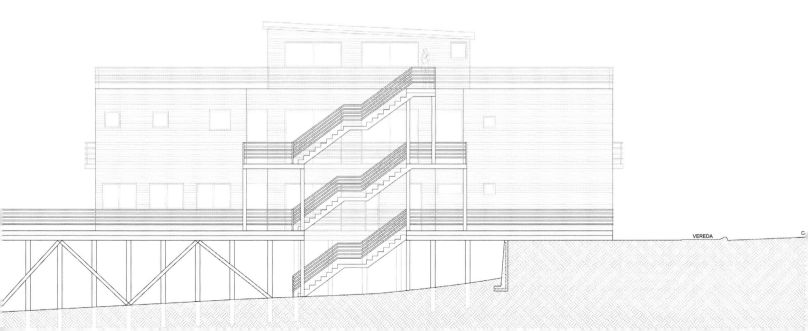

VEREDA

# Atra Doftana Hotel

## TECON
Valea Doftanei, Prahova, Romania
Photos: © Cosmin Dragomir

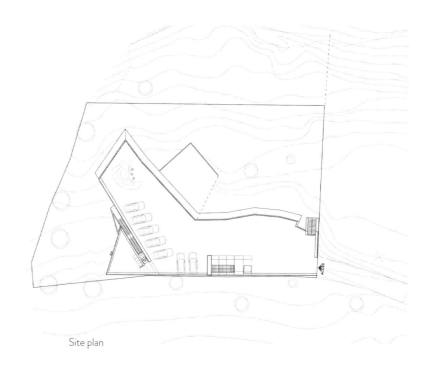

Site plan

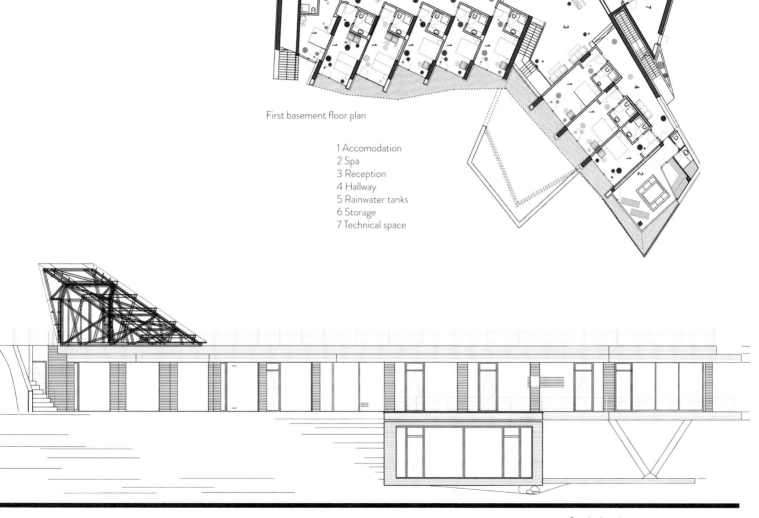

First basement floor plan

1 Accomodation
2 Spa
3 Reception
4 Hallway
5 Rainwater tanks
6 Storage
7 Technical space

South elevation

# ABaC Hotel

GCA Associated Architects
Barcelona, Spain
Photos © Hotel ABaC

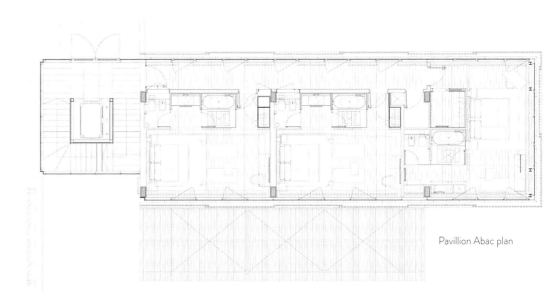

Pavillion Abac plan

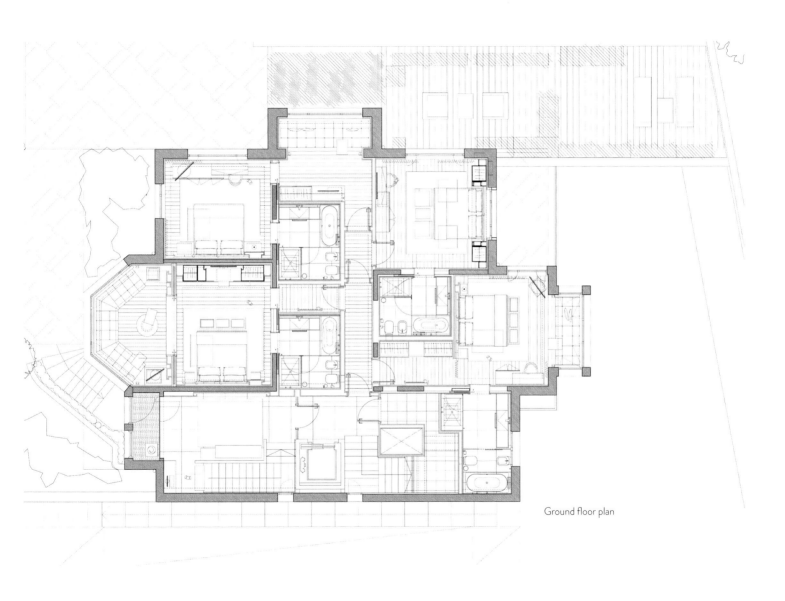

Ground floor plan

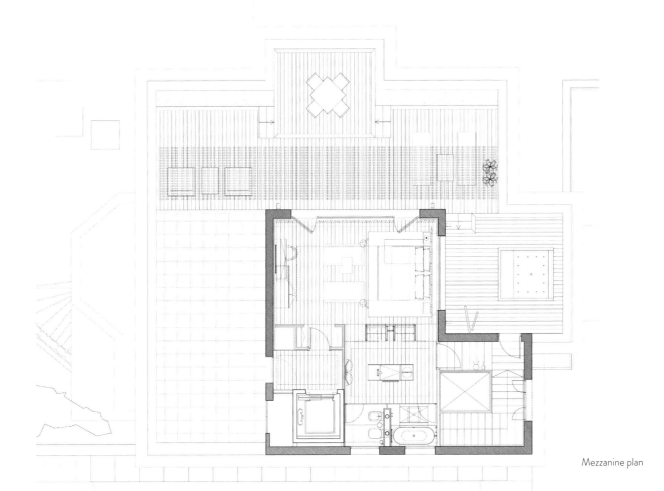

Mezzanine plan

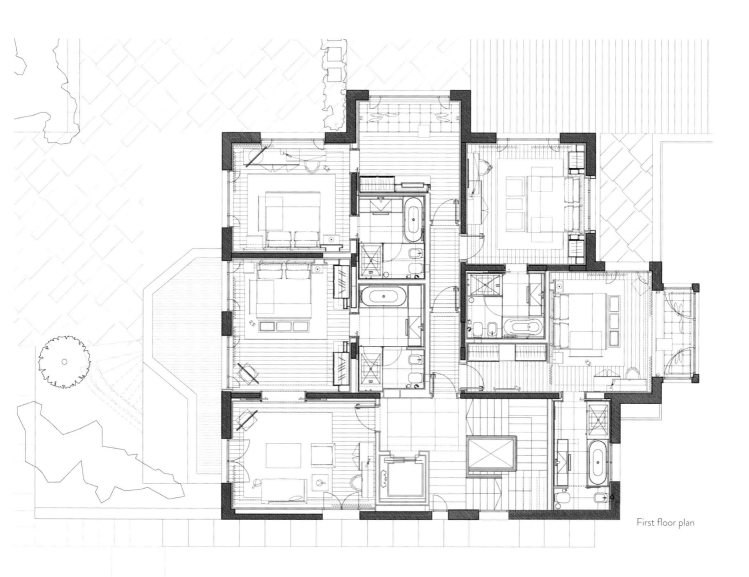

First floor plan

# Q Hotel

GRAFT Architects
Berlin, Germany
Photos © Hiepler Brunier Architekturfotografie

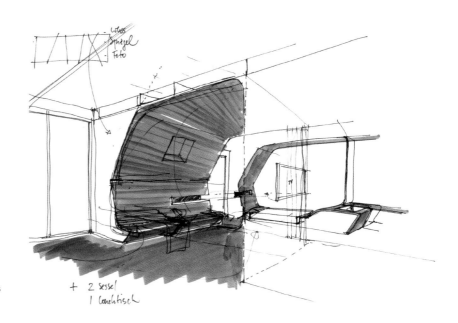

Sketches

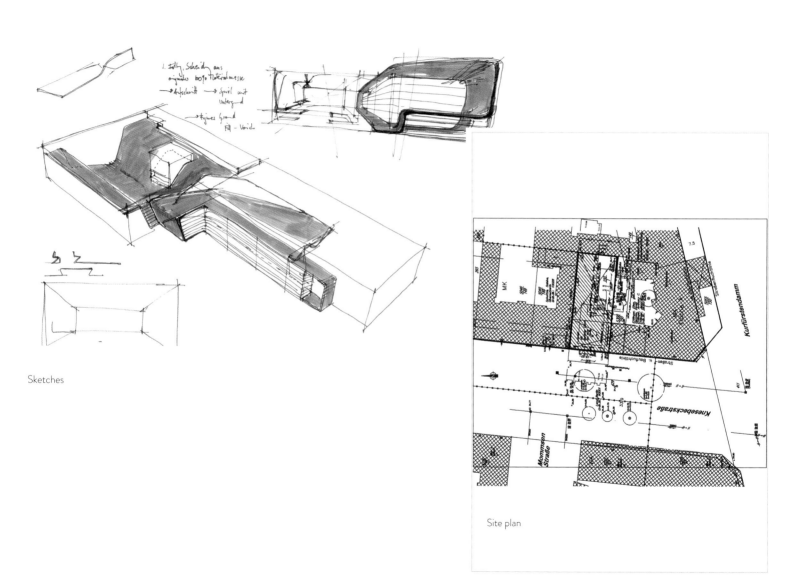

Sketches

Site plan

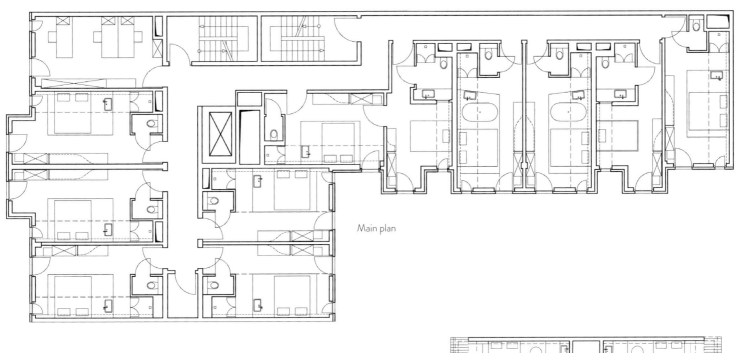

Main plan

Mezzanine plan

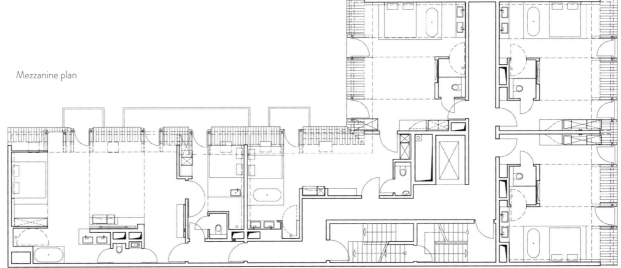

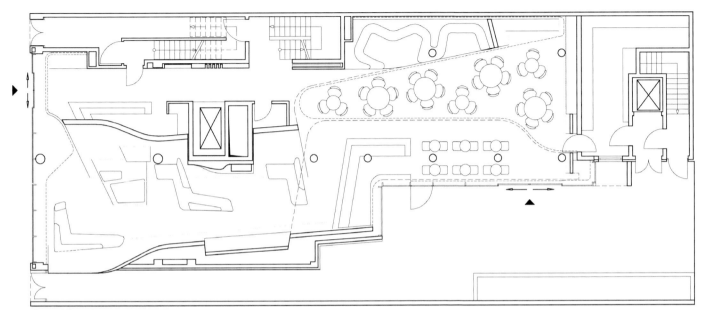

Ground floor plan

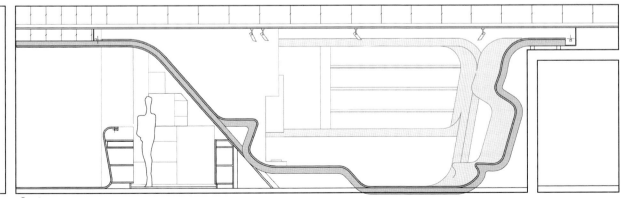

Sections

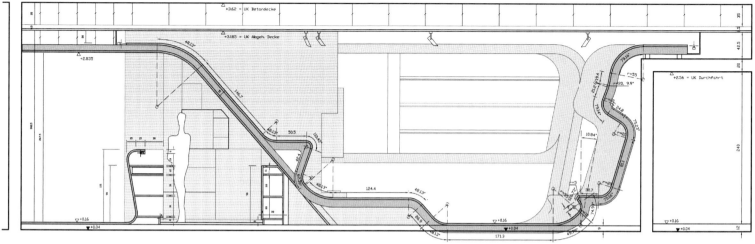

Sections

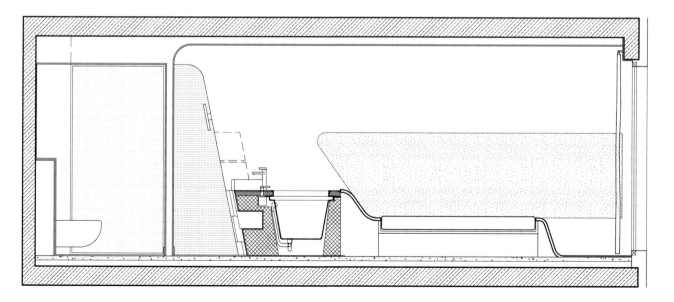

# The Mercure Eastgate Hotel

Blacksheep Architects
Oxford, England
Photos: © Gareth Gardner

Sketches of bar area and restaurant.

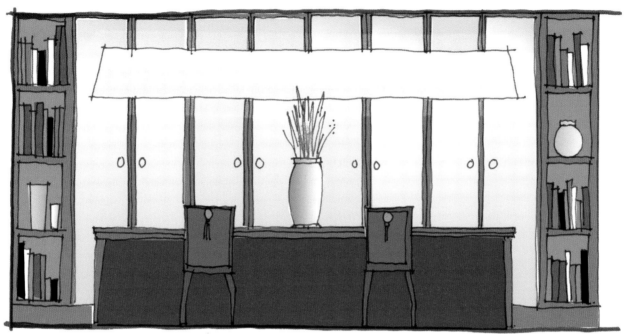

Reception sketch.

Sketches of bar area and restaurant.

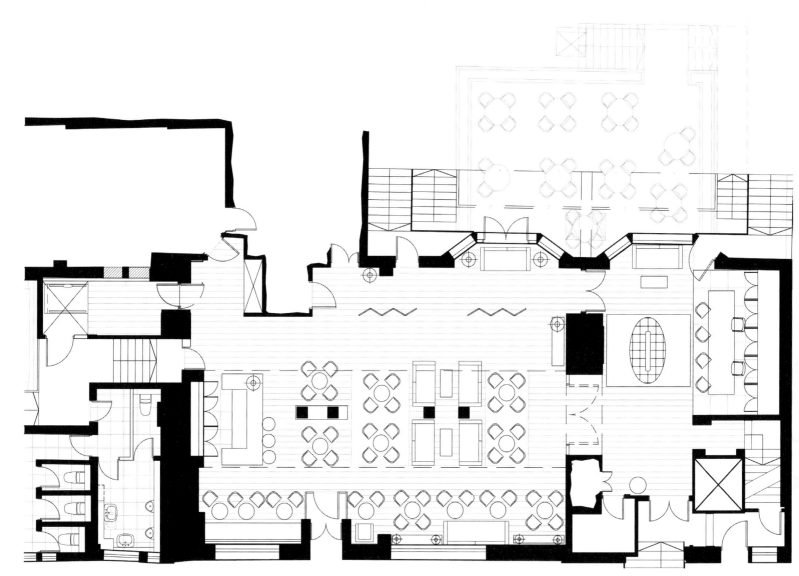

Bar floor plan

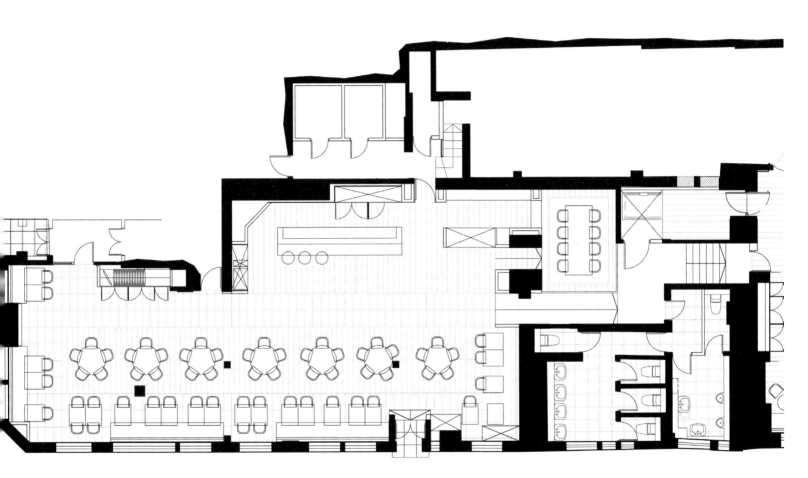

Restaurant floor plan

# Generator Venice

Massimo Roj Architects
Venice, Italy
Photos: © Nikolas Koenig

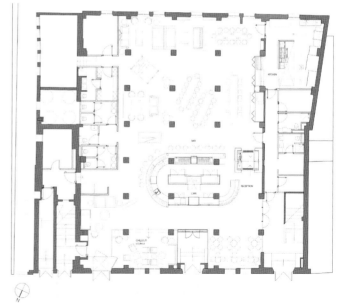

Ground floor plan

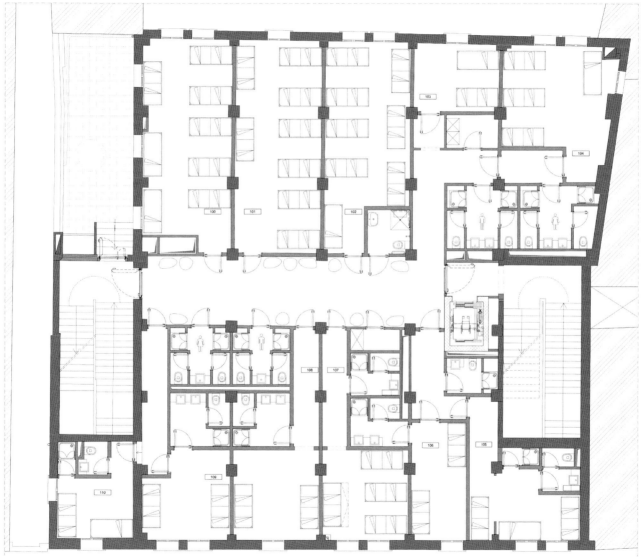

First floor plan

# Tre Merli Beach Hotel

Maurizio Bradaschia
Trieste, Italy
Photos: © Maurizio Bradaschia

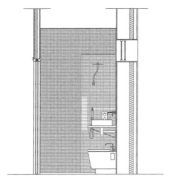
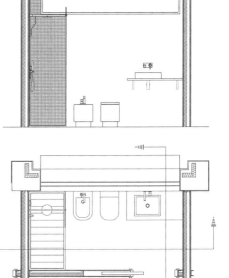

Plan and elevation of a room

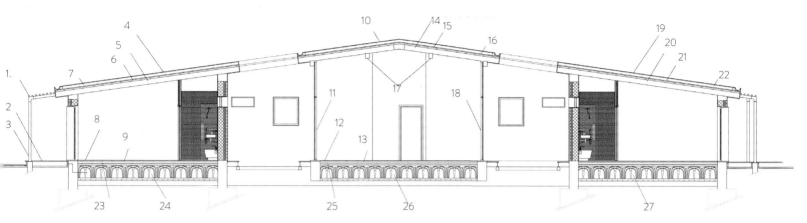

A-A Section

1. Teak slats shading, as shown approved by DL.
2. Teak table, as shown approved by DL
3. Pilar rectangular satin stainless steel (section 100x80x5 mm).
4. Coating aluminum painted green, as shown approved by DL.
5. Laminated wood beams painted in turquoise matte, as shown approved by DL
6. Wooden planks to man / woman painted teak mat, as shown approved by DL.
7. Expanded polystyrene panel microventilation.
8. Forged cement floor leveling resin finished helicopter (3 mm), as shown approved by DL.
9. Hood in the background.
10. Coating aluminum painted green, as shown approved by DL.
11. Opening of the glass wall of 100% H 250 cm soil
12. Teak wood flooring, as shown approved by DL.
13. Ground.

14. Glulam beams varnished teak, as shown approved by DL.
15. Plank wood varnished teak, as shown approved by DL.
16. Microventilado Panel expanded polystyrene.
17. Laminated wood beams painted teak, as shown approved by DL.
18. Glass wall opening to 100% H 250 cm of soil.
19. Coating aluminum painted green, as shown approved by DL.
20. Glulam beams varnished teak, as shown approved by DL.
21. Plank wood varnished teak, as shown approved by DL.
22. Microventilado Panel expanded polystyrene.
23. Insulating in the CIS and expanded clay.
24. Ventilation.
25. Insulating in the CIS and expanded clay.
26. Ventilation.

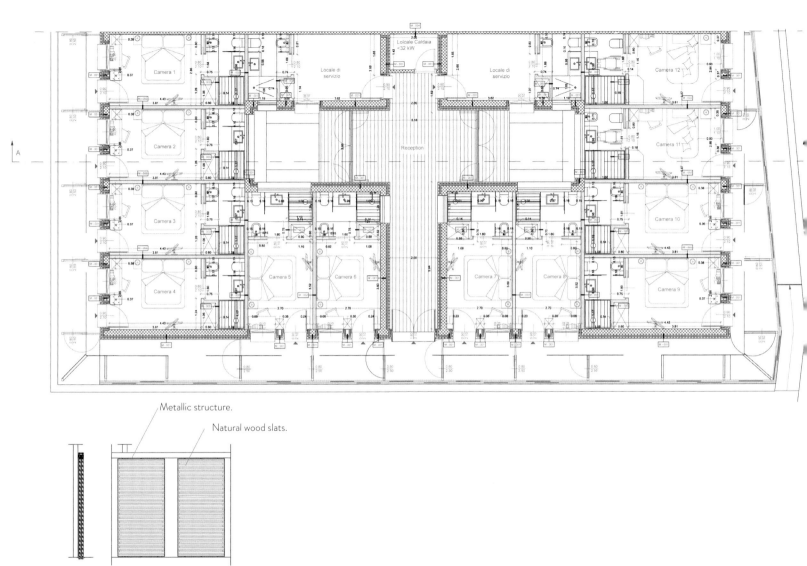

Metallic structure.

Natural wood slats.

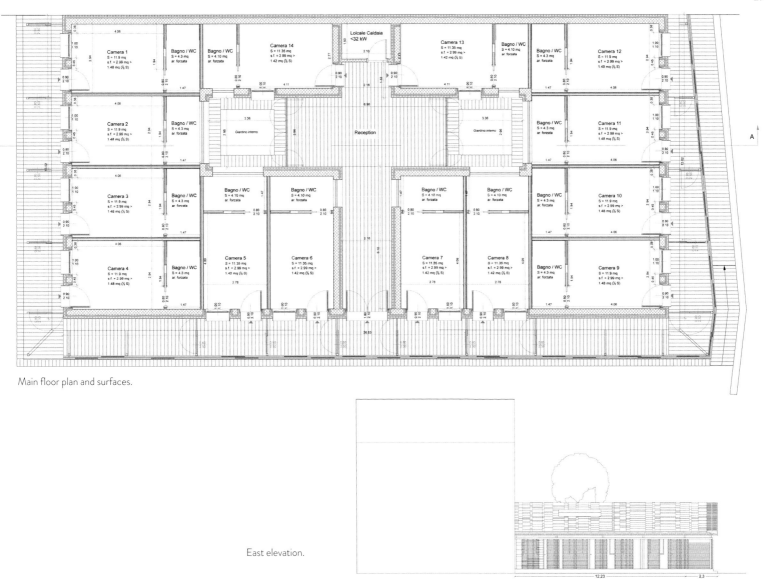

Main floor plan and surfaces.

East elevation.

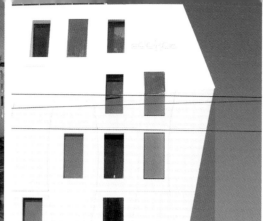

# Seekoo Hotel

King Kong Architecture Workshop
Bordeaux, France
Photos © Arthur Péquin

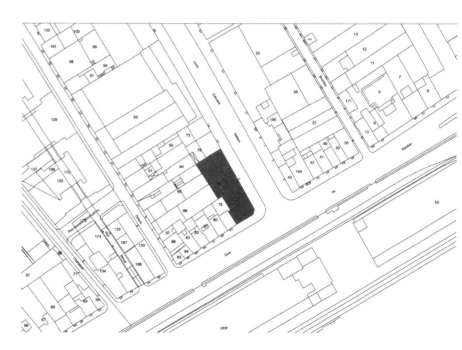

Sitemap plan

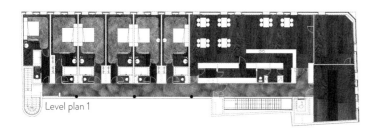

Level plan 1

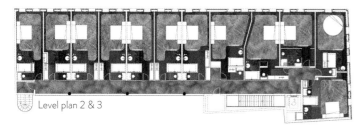

Level plan 2 & 3

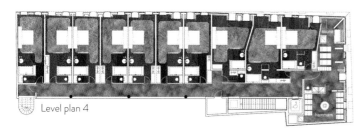

Level plan 4

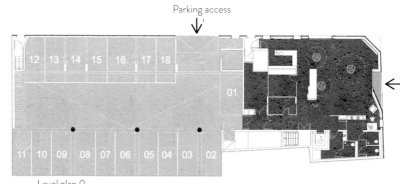

Parking access

Level plan 0

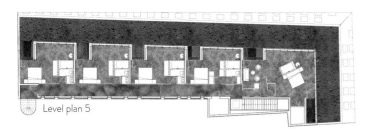

Level plan 5

Floor plans

# Generator Amsterdam

Idea (Integrated Disciplines of Engineering and Architecture)
Patagonia Occidental, Magallanes, Chile
Photos: © Nikolas Koenig

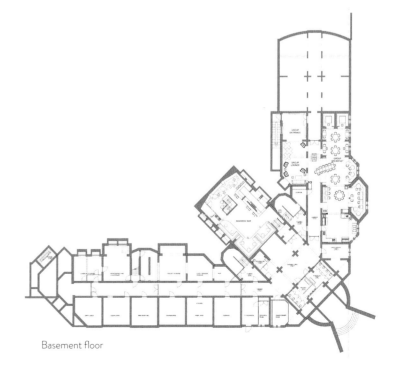

Basement floor

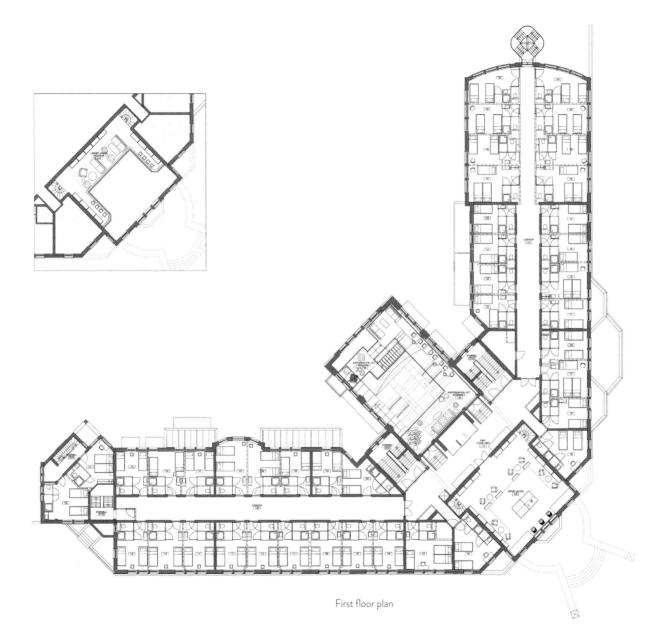

First floor plan

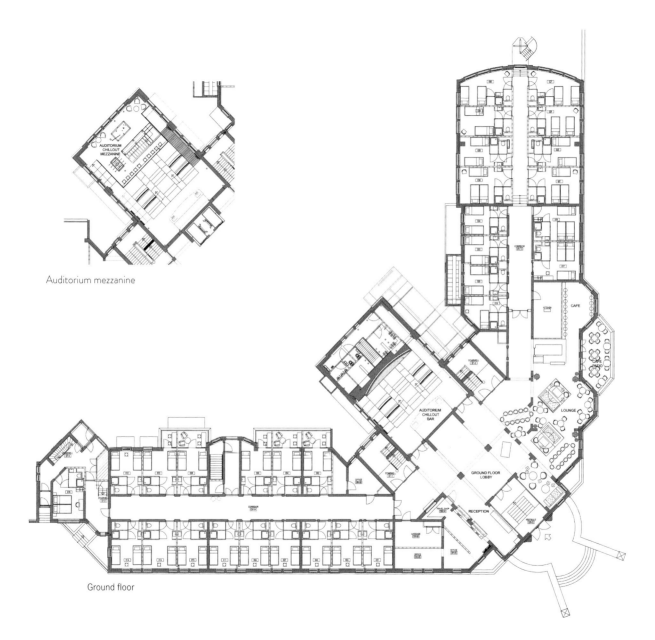

Auditorium mezzanine

Ground floor

# Bayside Marina Hotel

Yasutaka Yoshimura Architects
Kanagawa, Japan
Photos: © Yasutaka Yoshimura Architects

2.428

2.428

BED ROOM

2ND FLOOR PLAN

LIVING

BATH ROOM

12.192

Maisonette type 1st & 2nd floor plan.

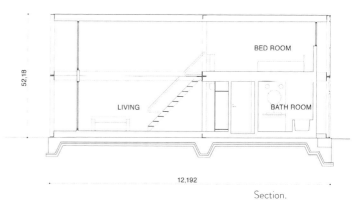

52,18

BED ROOM

LIVING

BATH ROOM

12.192

Section.

Main floor plan.

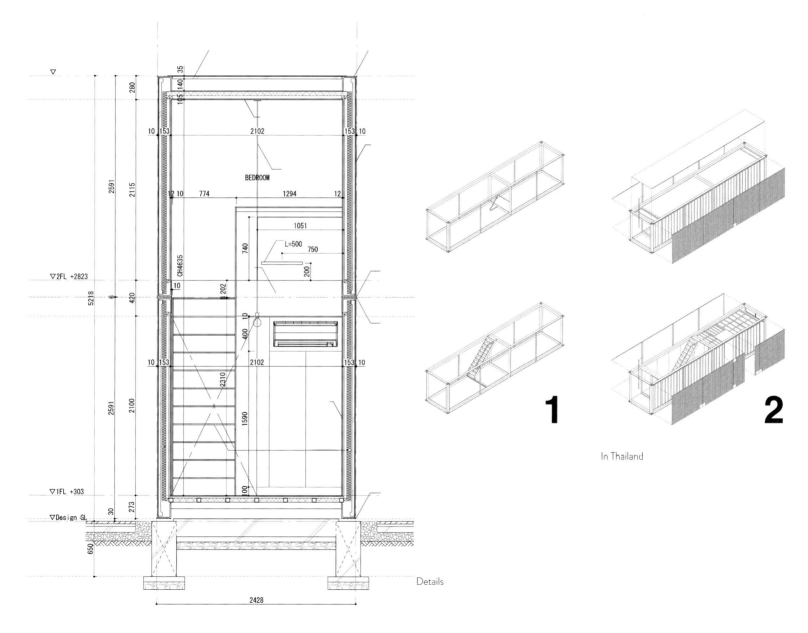

BEDROOM

L=500

▽2FL +2823

CH4635

▽1FL +303

▽Design GL

35
280
105 140
10 153
2102
153 10
12 10
774
1294
12
1051
740
750
200
10
202
360
400
2310
2102
153 10
1590
100
2591
2115
5218
6
420
2100
2591
30
273
650
2428

In Thailand

1

2

Details

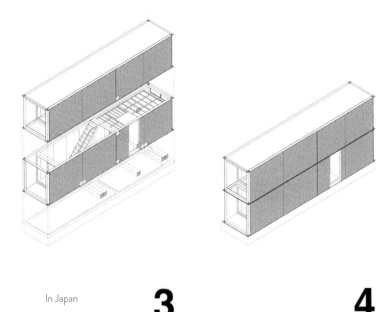

In Japan

# 3

# 4

1. Twistlock.
2. Anchored.
3. Diaphram St. PL-25 SS400 (Corner casting hole).
4. St. L-175x175x12.
5. Nut.
6. Washer.
7. Diaphram St.PL-25 SS400 (Medium bolt hole) (Corner casting hole).
8. Spacer St.PL-6 SS400 (Medium bolt hole) (Corner casting hole).

9. Diaphram St.PL-25 SS400 (Medium bolt hole) (Corner casting hole).
10. Medium bolt M16.
11. Protective cap double nut.
12. Washer.
13. Diaphram St. PL-25 SS400 (Anchor bolt hole) (Corner casting hole).
14. Leveling mortar t30.
15. Anchor bolt M12.
16. Continous foundation.

# Explora Patagonia Hotel

Germán del Sol
Patagonia Occidental, Magallanes, Chile
Photos © Guy Wemborne

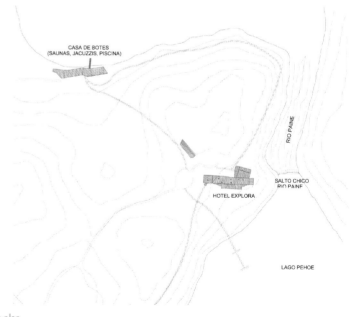

Location plan

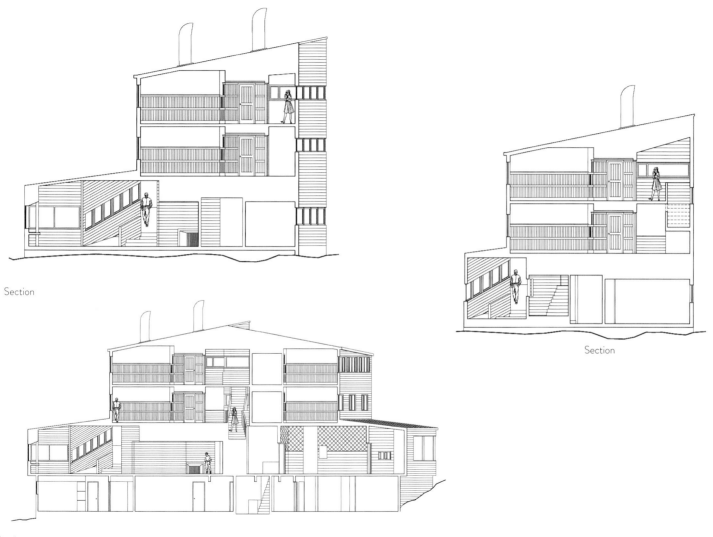

Section

Section

Section

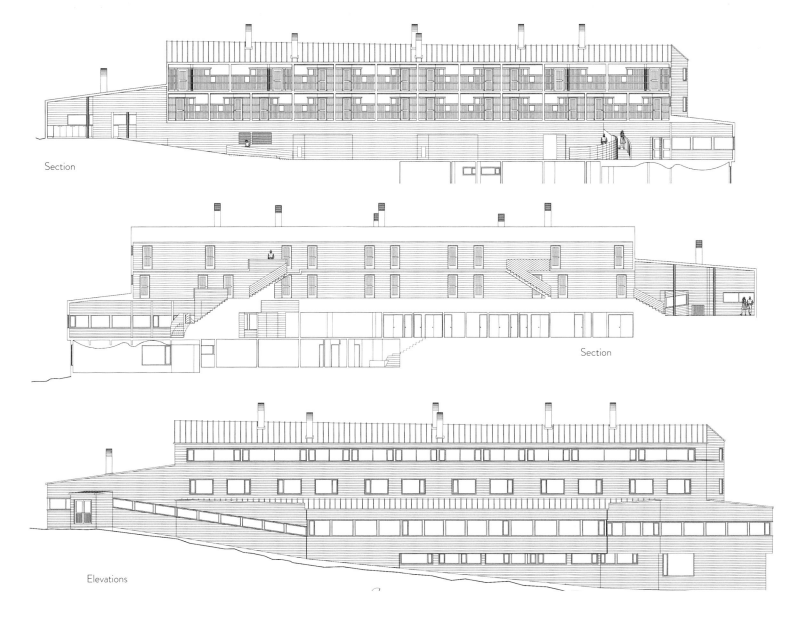

Section

Section

Elevations

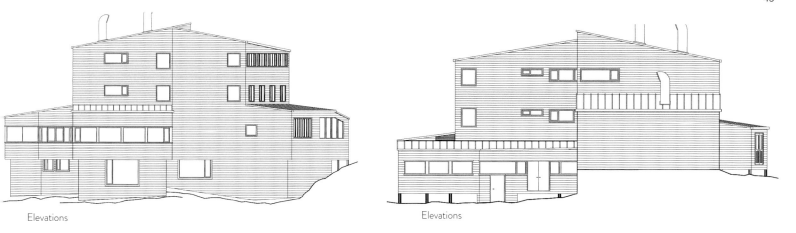

Elevations

Elevations

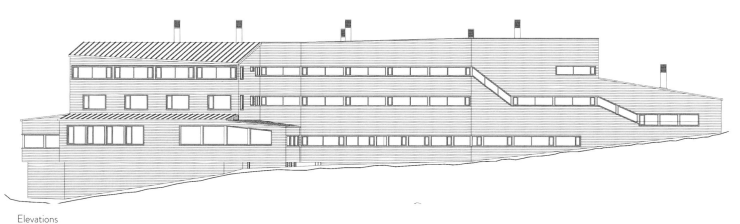

Elevations

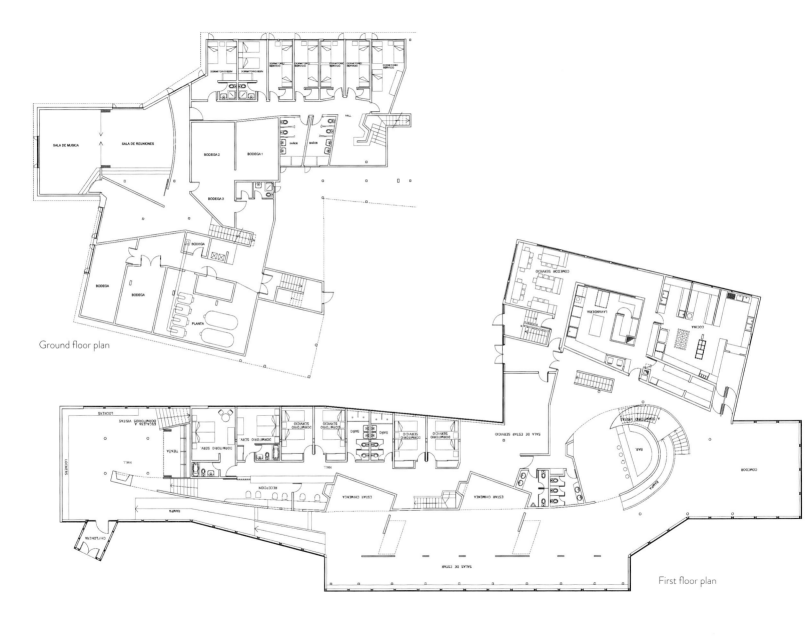

Ground floor plan

First floor plan

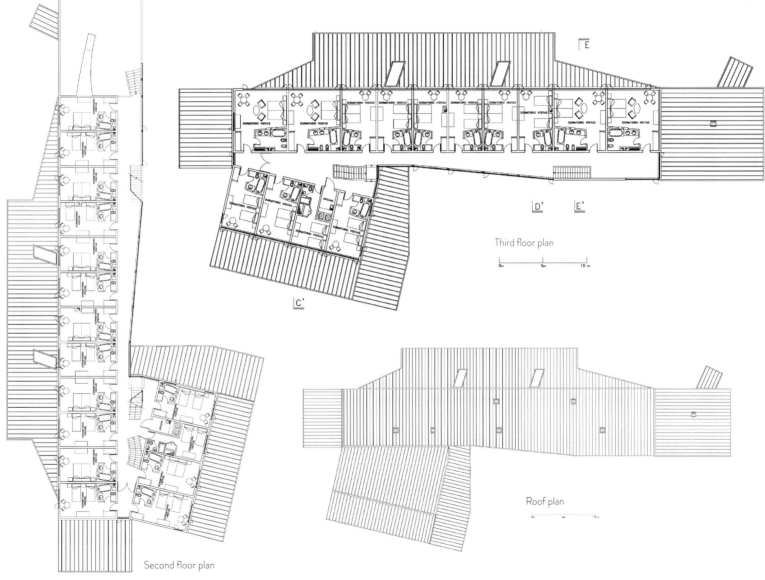

Third floor plan

0m    5m    10m

Second floor plan

Roof plan

# Turtagrø Hotel

Jarmund/Vigsnæs AS Architects
Sognefjellet, Norway
Photos © Nils Petter Dahle

Location plan

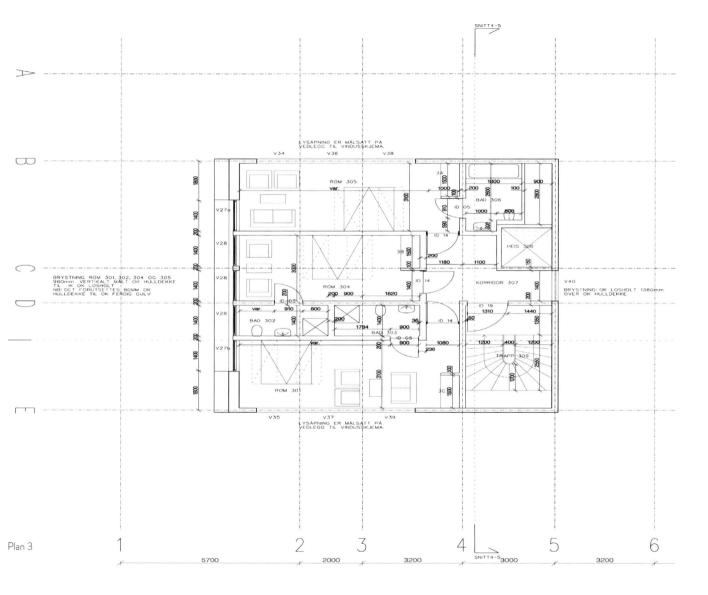

SNITT 4 - 5

LYSÅPNING ER MÅLSATT PÅ
VEDLEGG TIL VINDUSSKJEMA.

V34        V36        V38

ROM 305

BRYSTNING ROM 301, 302, 304 OG 305
980mm VERTIKALT MÅLT OK HULLDEKKE
TIL IK OK LOSHOLT
NB! DET FORUTSETTES 80MM OK
HULLDEKKE TIL OK FERDIG GULV

V27

V28

V28

V28

V27

BAD 306

HEIS 308

ROM 304

BAD 302

BAD 303

KORRIDOR 307

V40

BRYSTNING OK LOSHOLT 1380mm
OVER OK HULLDEKKE

ROM 301

TRAPP 309

V35        V37        V39

LYSÅPNING ER MÅLSATT PÅ
VEDLEGG TIL VINDUSSKJEMA.

ID 05
ID 14
ID 14
ID 05
ID 19
ID 14
ID 05

Plan 3

1        2        3        4        5        6

SNITT 4 - 5

5700        2000        3200        3000        3200

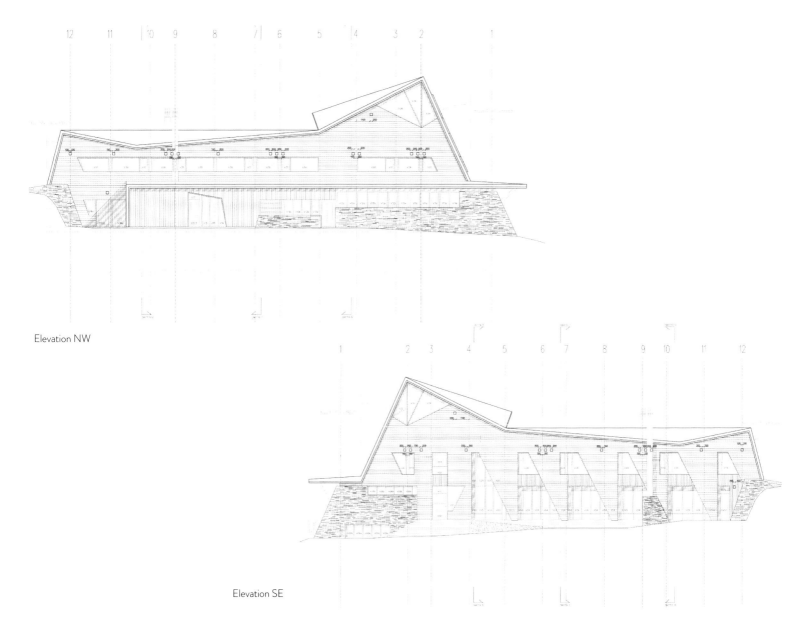

Elevation NW

Elevation SE

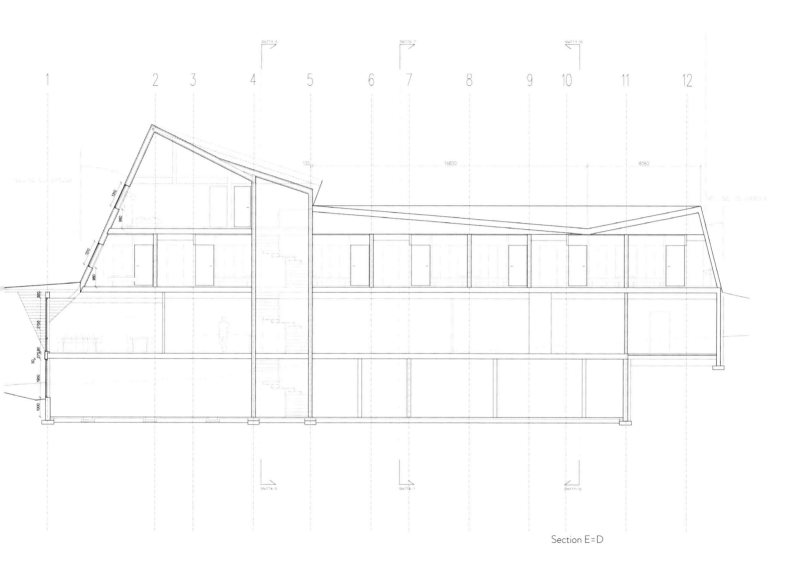

Section E=D

# Kassel Grimm Hotel

Mohen Design International
Shanghai, China
Photos © Maoder Chou

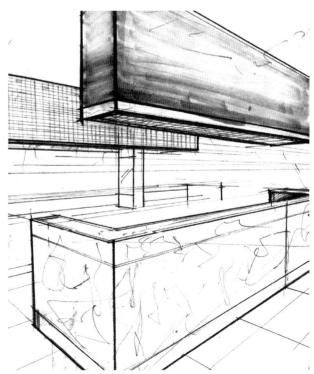

Reception sketch

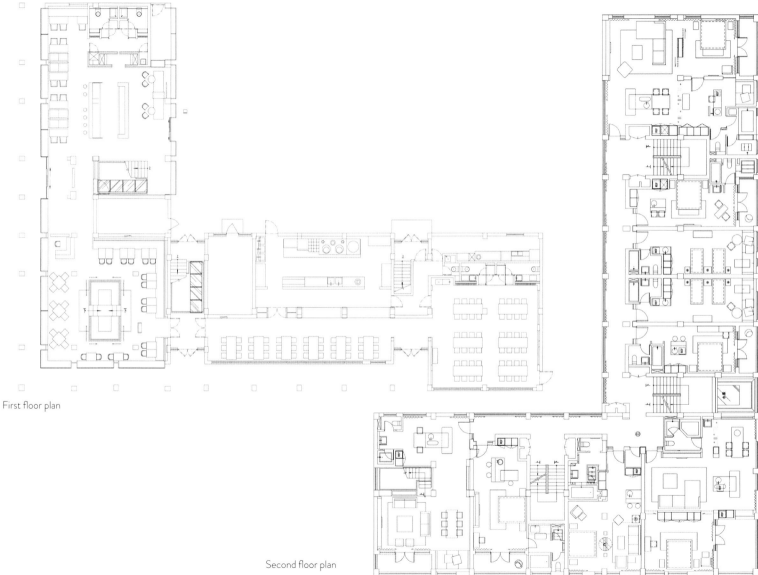

First floor plan

Second floor plan

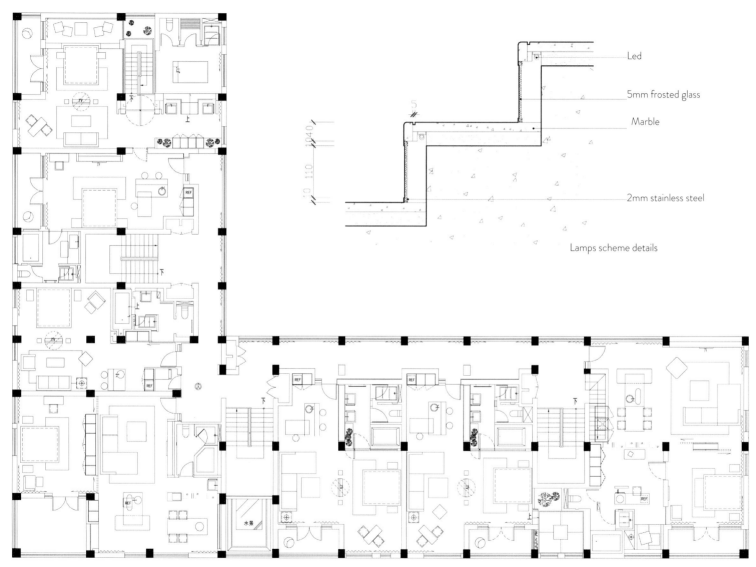

Led

5mm frosted glass

Marble

2mm stainless steel

Lamps scheme details

Third floor plan

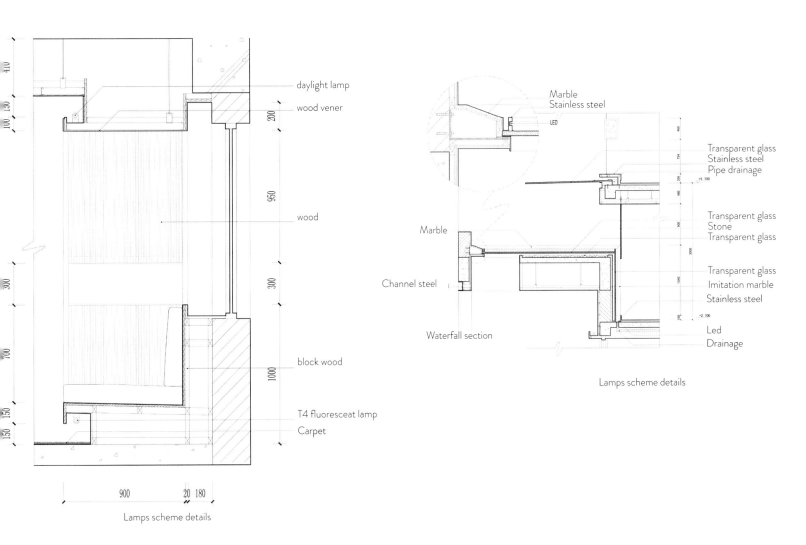

daylight lamp

wood vener

wood

block wood

T4 fluresceat lamp

Carpet

Lamps scheme details

Marble
Stainless steel

LED

Marble

Channel steel

Waterfall section

Transparent glass
Stainless steel
Pipe drainage

Transparent glass
Stone
Transparent glass

Transparent glass
Imitation marble

Stainless steel

Led
Drainage

Lamps scheme details

# La Buena Vida Hostel

ARCO Contemporary Architecture
José Lew Kirsch, Bernardo Lew Kirsch
Ciudad de Mexico, Mexico
Photos © Jaime Navarro

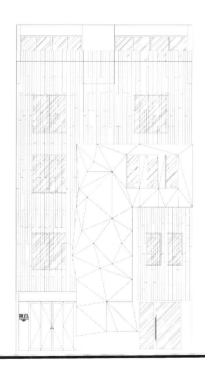

Main facade

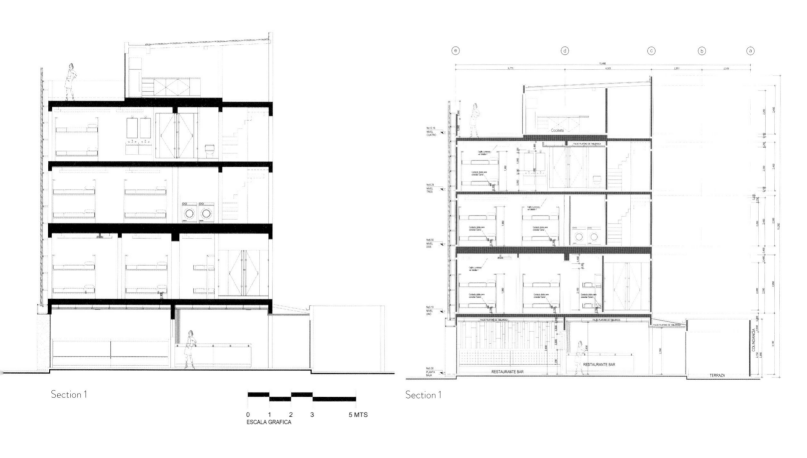

Section 1

Section 1

0 1 2 3 5 MTS
ESCALA GRAFICA

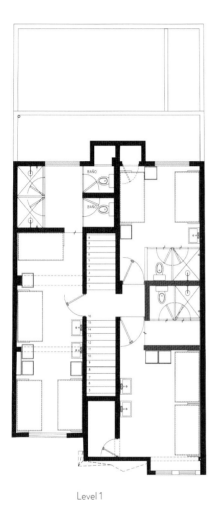

Level 1

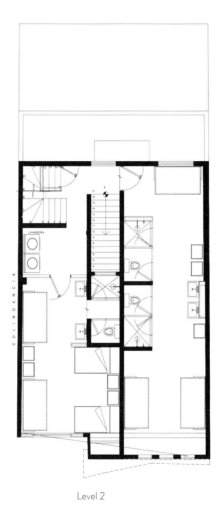

Level 2

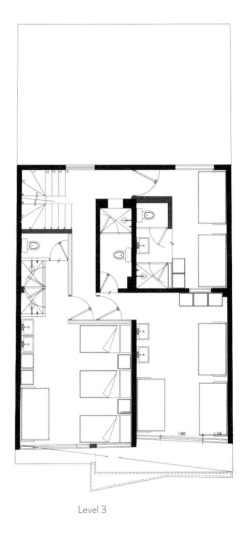

Level 3

0   1   2   3        5 MTS
ESCALA GRAFICA

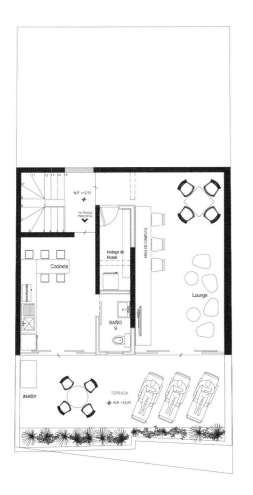

Level 4

Section 3

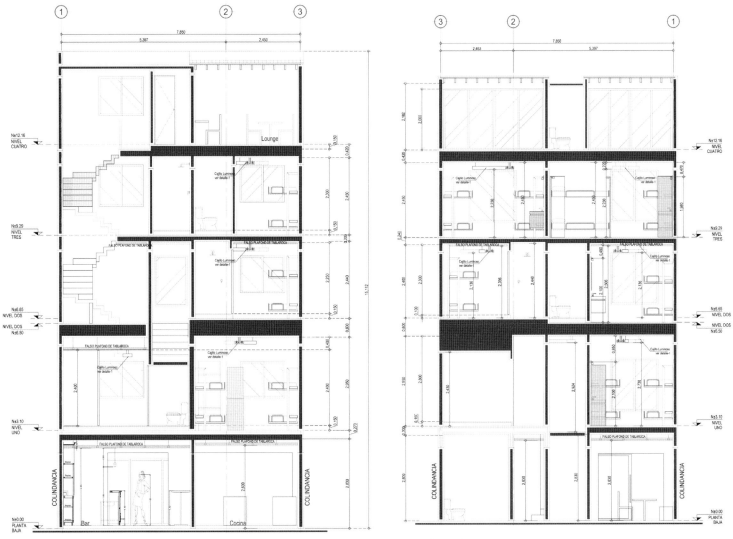

Section 4

Section 5

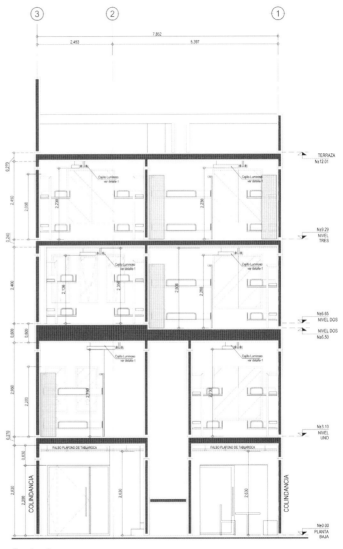

Section 6

# Generator Barcelona

Ibinser
Barcelona, Spain
Photos © Nikolas Koenig

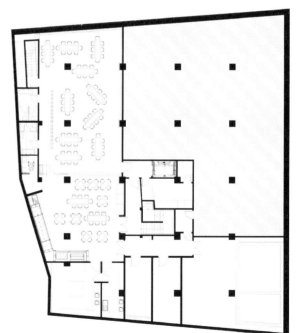

Basement plan

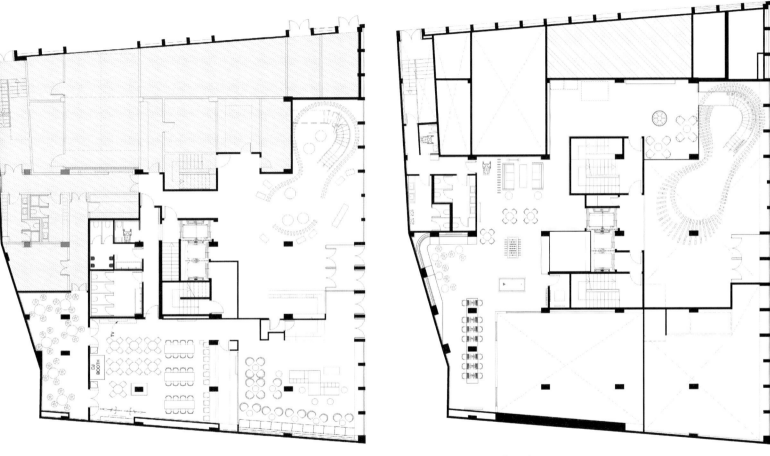

Ground floor plan

Mezzanine floor plan

# Southern Ocean Lodge

Max Pritchard Architect
Kangaroo Island, South Australia
Photos: © George Apostolidis, Sam Noonan

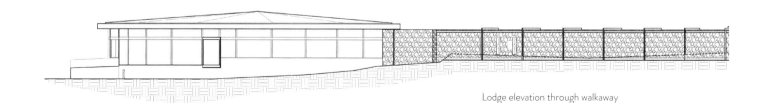

Lodge elevation through walkaway

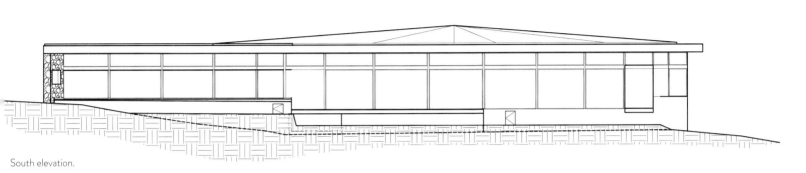

South elevation.

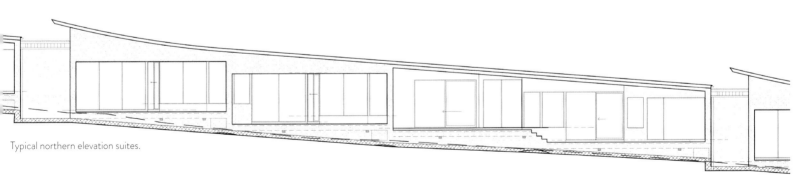

Typical northern elevation suites.

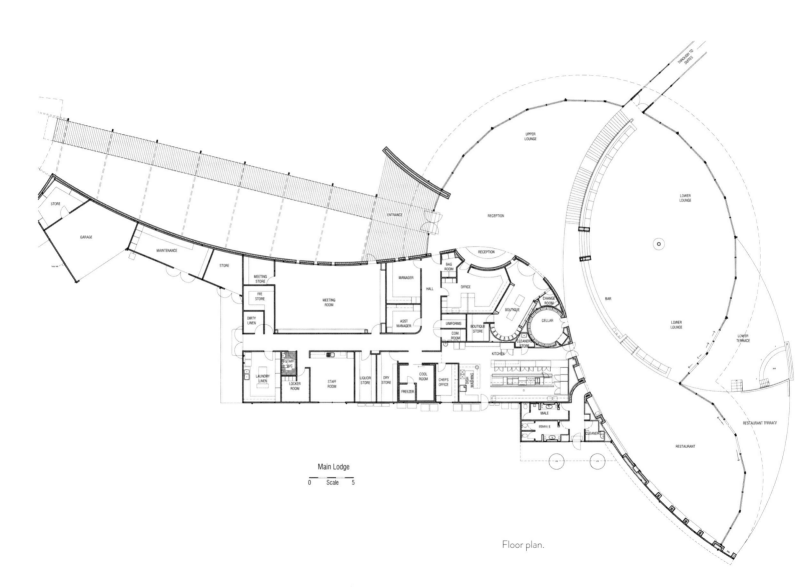

STORE

GARAGE

MAINTENANCE

STORE

ENTRANCE

RECEPTION

UPPER
LOUNGE

LOWER
LOUNGE

THROUGH TO
SUITES

MEETING
STORE

FFE
STORE

MEETING
ROOM

DIRTY
LINEN

MANAGER

HALL

ASST
MANAGER

RECEPTION

BAG
ROOM

OFFICE

BOUTIQUE

CHANGE
ROOM

CELLAR

BAR

LOWER
LOUNGE

LOWER
TERRACE

UNIFORMS

COM
ROOM

BOUTIQUE
STORE

CLEANERS
STORE

STAFF
WC

LAUNDRY
LINEN

LOCKER
ROOM

STAFF
ROOM

LIQUOR
STORE

DRY
STORE

COOL
ROOM

FREEZER

CHEF'S
OFFICE

DISH
WASHING

KITCHEN

MALE

FEMALE

CLEANERS

RESTAURANT
TERRACE

RESTAURANT

Main Lodge

0    Scale    5

Floor plan.

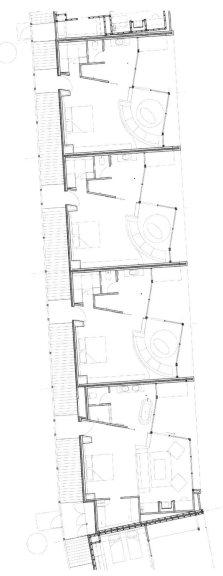

Typical floor plan suites.

# Grace Santorini Hotel

Divercity & Mplusm
Santorini, Greece
Photos: © Erieta Attali & Serge Detalle

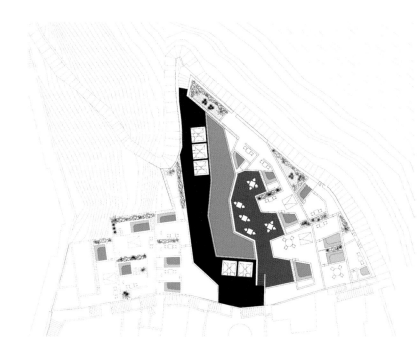

Location plan

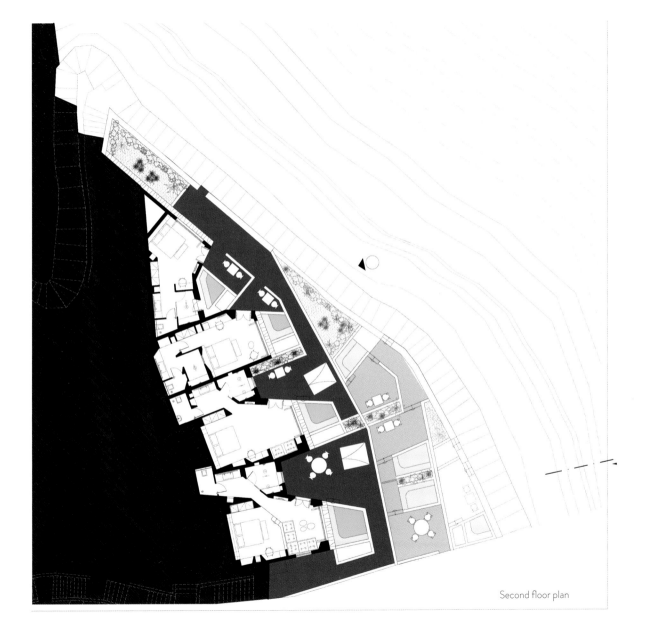

Second floor plan

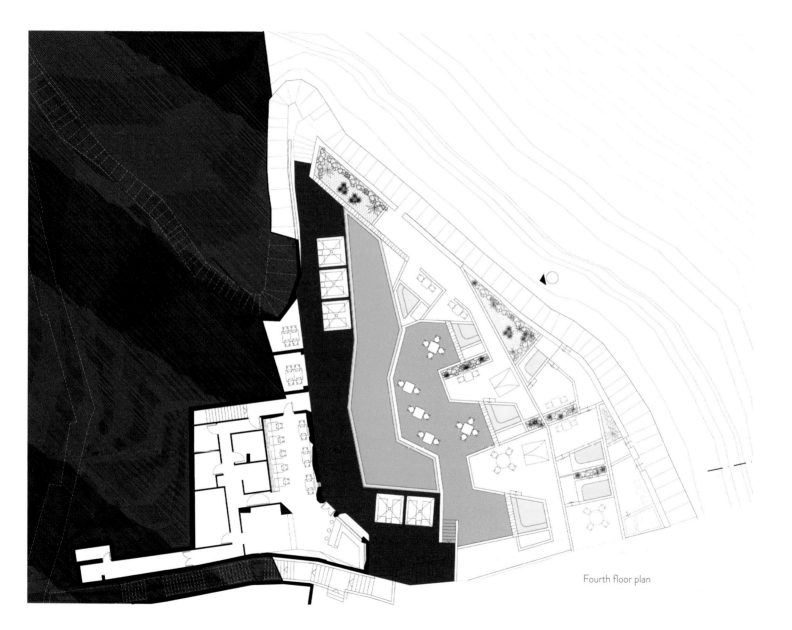

Fourth floor plan

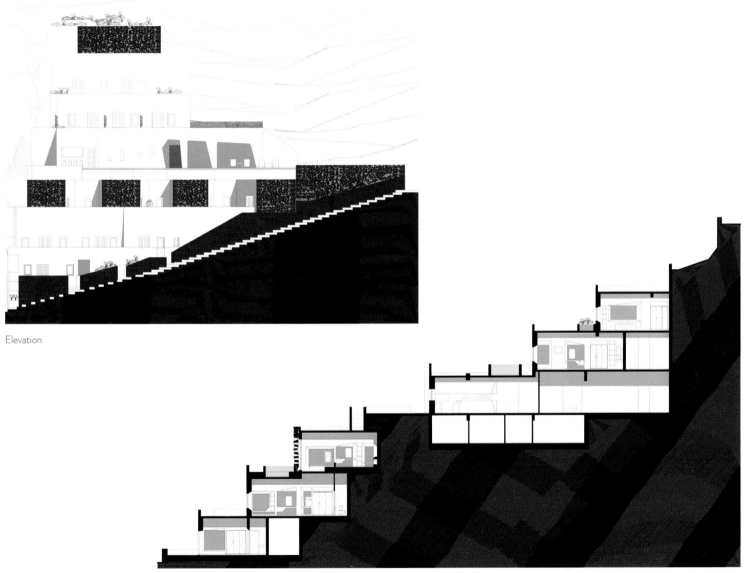

Elevation

Section

# W Barcelona Hotel

Ricardo Bofill Architecture Workshop
Barcelona, Spain
Photos: © Lluis Carbonell, Gregori Civera

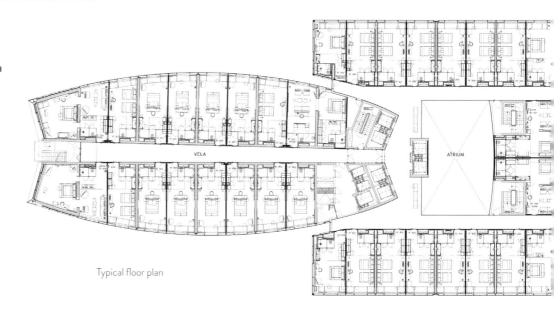

Typical floor plan

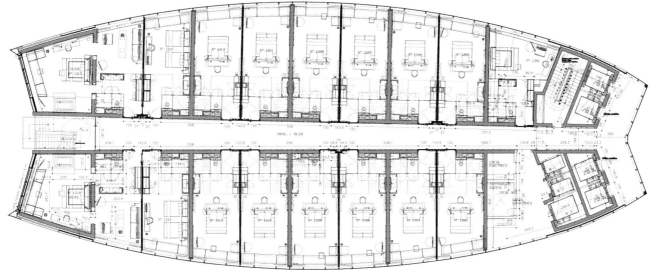

Twelfth floor plan

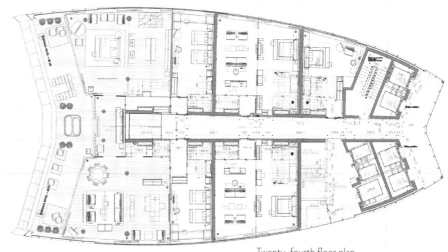

Twenty-fourth floor plan

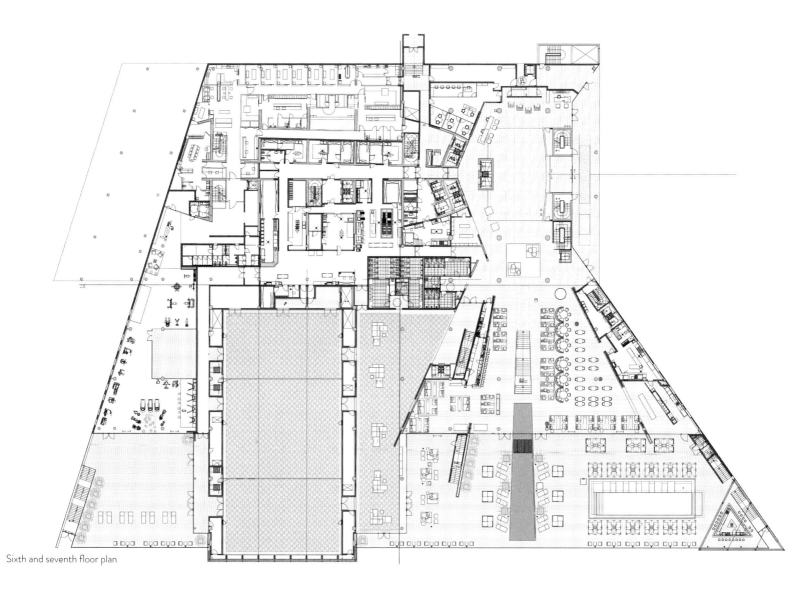

Sixth and seventh floor plan

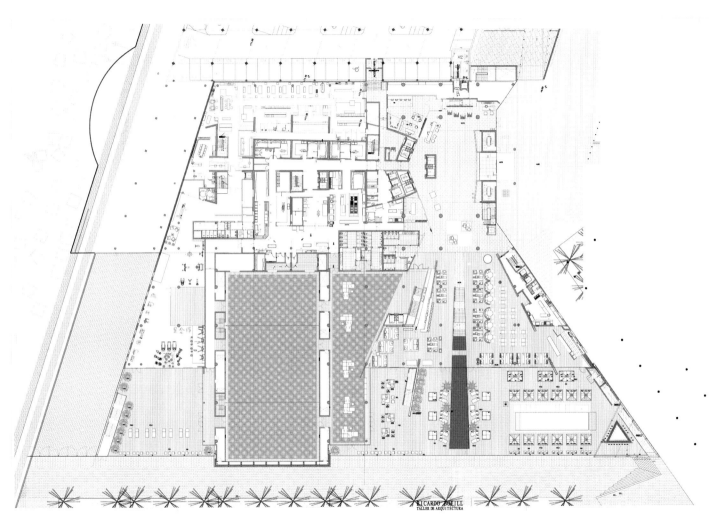

Ground floor plan

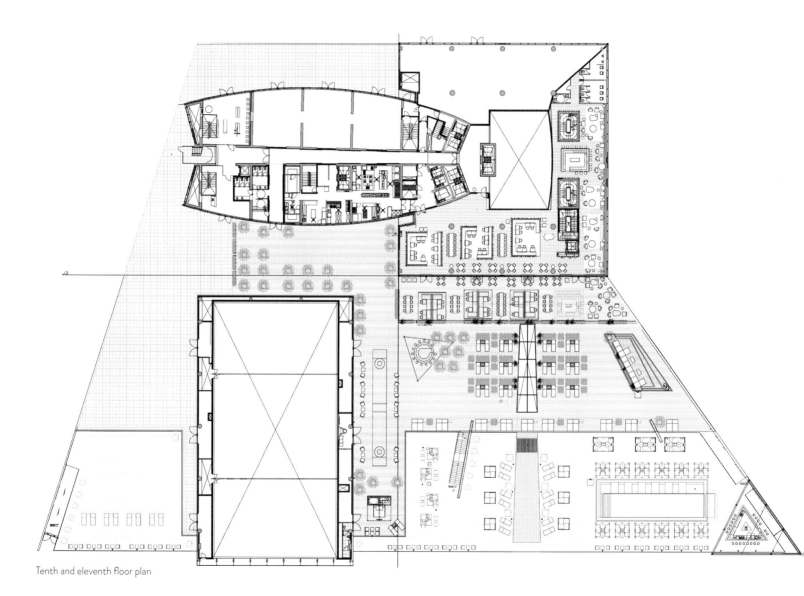

Tenth and eleventh floor plan

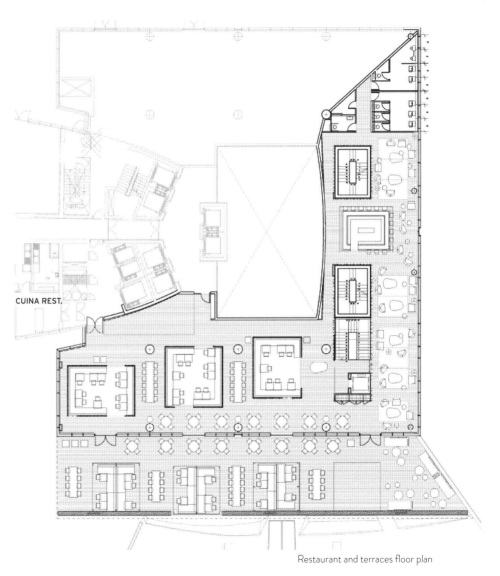

CUINA REST.

Restaurant and terraces floor plan

# The Mirror Hotel

GCA Associated Architects
Barcelona, Spain
Photos: © Marco Pastori & Jordi Miralles (façade)

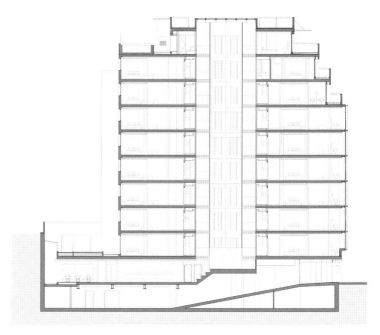

Main section

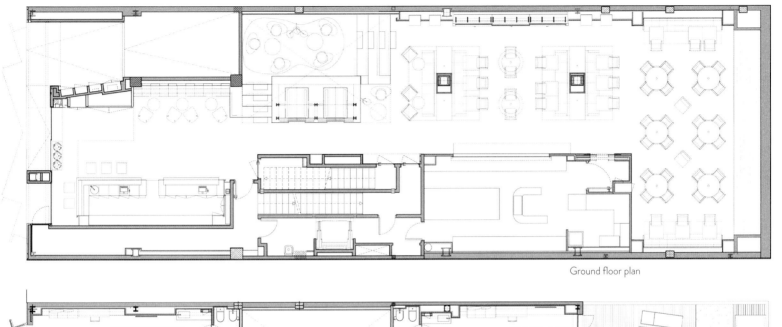

Ground floor plan

First floor plan

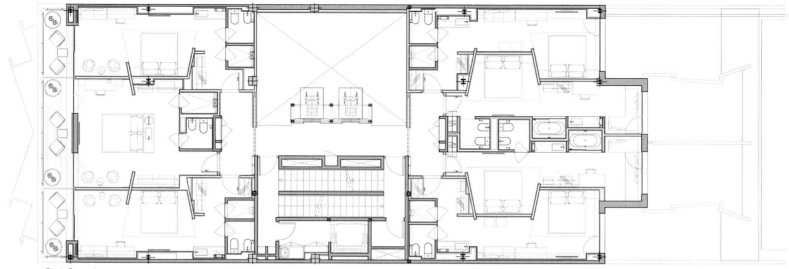

Sixth floor plan

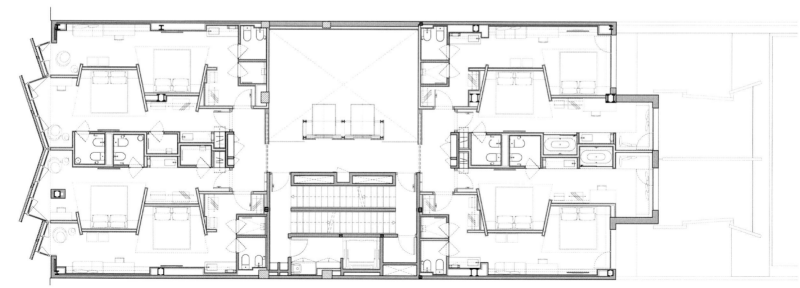

Sample floor plan

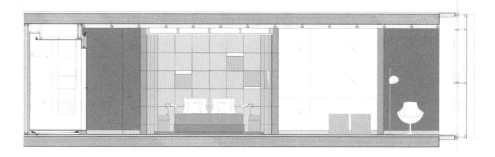

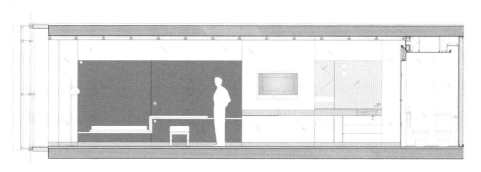

Sample room section

# Emperor Hotel

**GRAFT Architects**
Beijing, China
Photos: © L2 STUDIOR

1. Dining area
2. Lounge area
3. VIP room
4. Bar
5. Kitchen
6. Storage
7. Reception
8. Uni-sex toilet
9. Kitchen
10. Staff Canteen
11. Staff Locker
12. Office

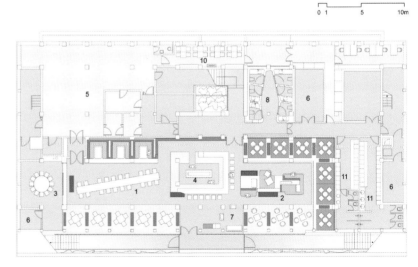

Basement plan

1. Main reception
2. Standard room
3. Deluxe room
4. Junior Suite
5. Secondary reception
6. Extension room
7. Storage
8. Security room
9. Shop

Floor plan

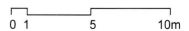

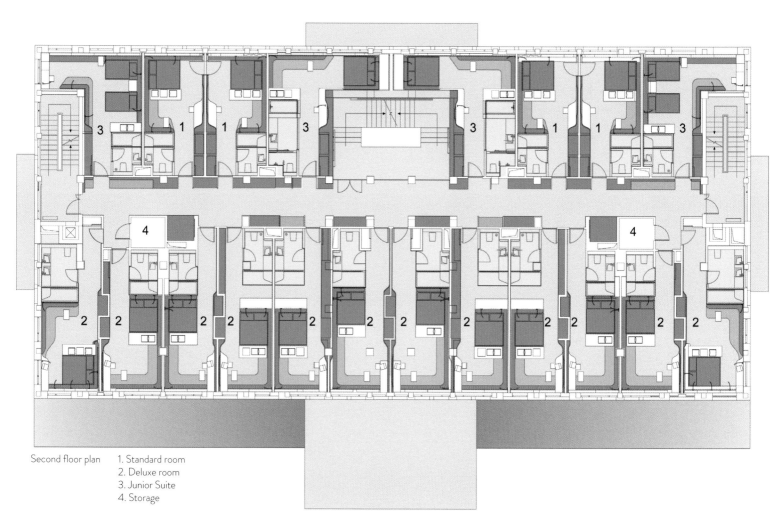

Second floor plan    1. Standard room
                     2. Deluxe room
                     3. Junior Suite
                     4. Storage

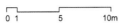

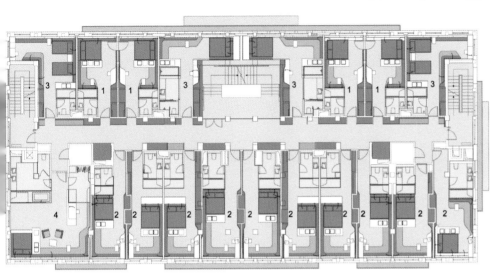

1. Standard room
2. Deluxe room
3. Junior Suite
4. Suite
5. Storage

Third floor plan

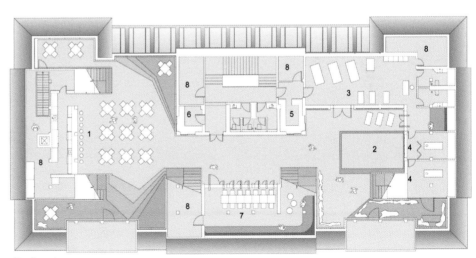

1. Bar area
2. Spa area
3. Fitness room
4. Massage room
5. Juice bar
6. Foodstand
7. Meeting room
8. Storage

Rooftop plan

# Iveria Hotel

GRAFT-Gesellschaft von Architects
Tbilisi, Georgia
Photos: © Hiepler & Brunier Architekturfotografie, Tobias Hein

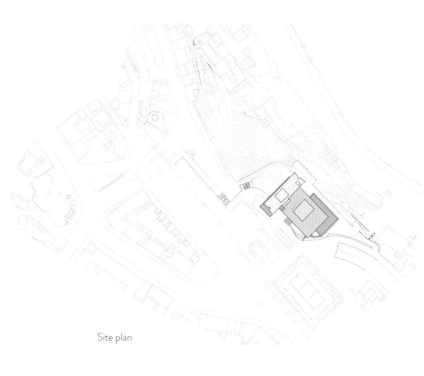

Site plan

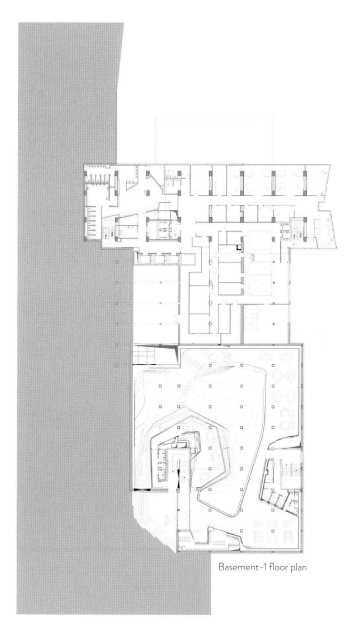

Basement-1 floor plan

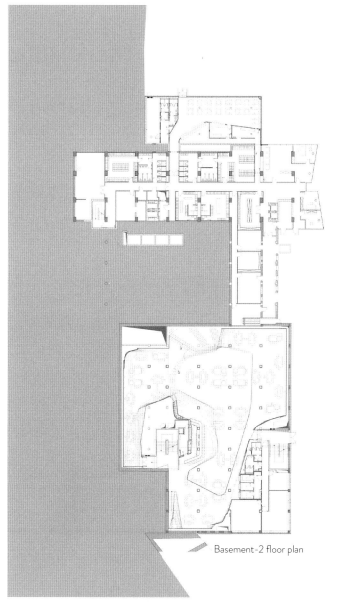

Basement-2 floor plan

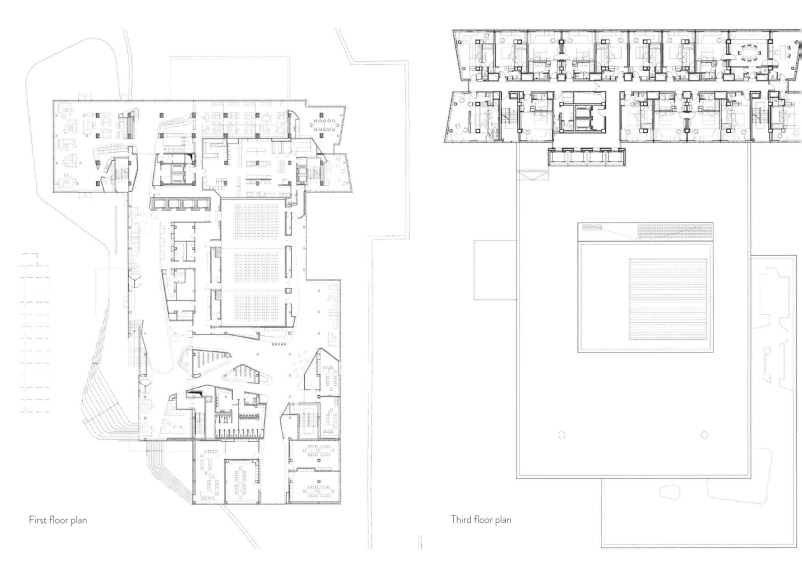

First floor plan

Third floor plan

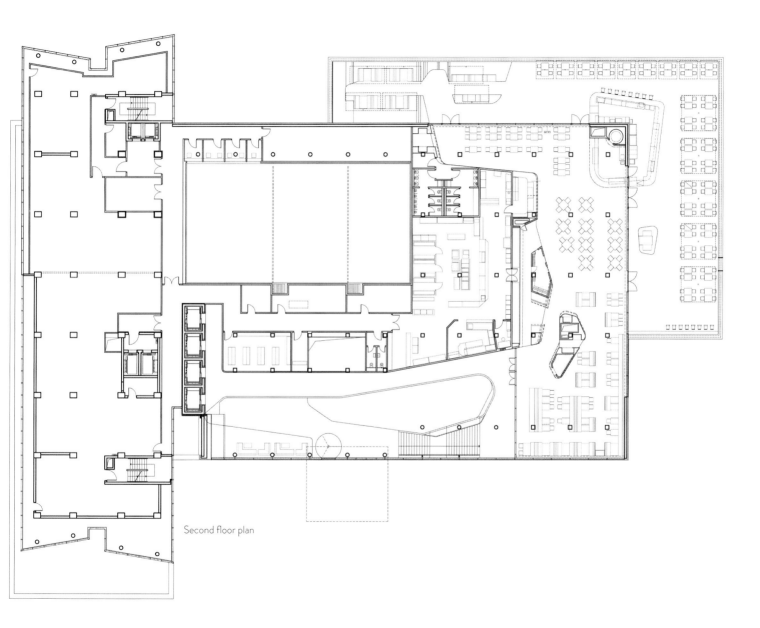

Second floor plan

# URBN Hotel

A00 Architects
Shanghai, China
Photos: © Nacása & Partners Inc.

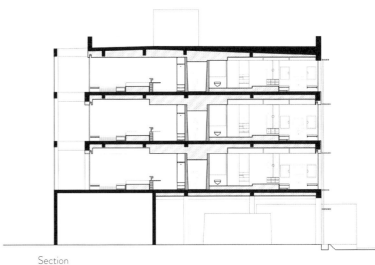

Section

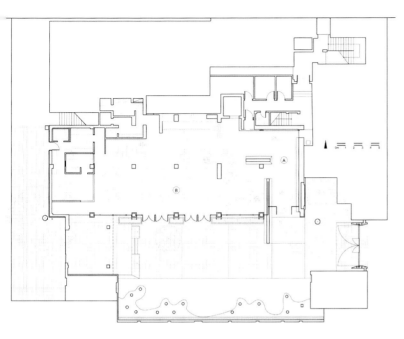

Ground floor plan
A Reception
B Roomtwentyeight

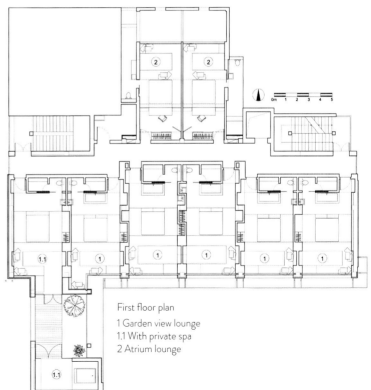

First floor plan

1 Garden view lounge
1.1 With private spa
2 Atrium lounge

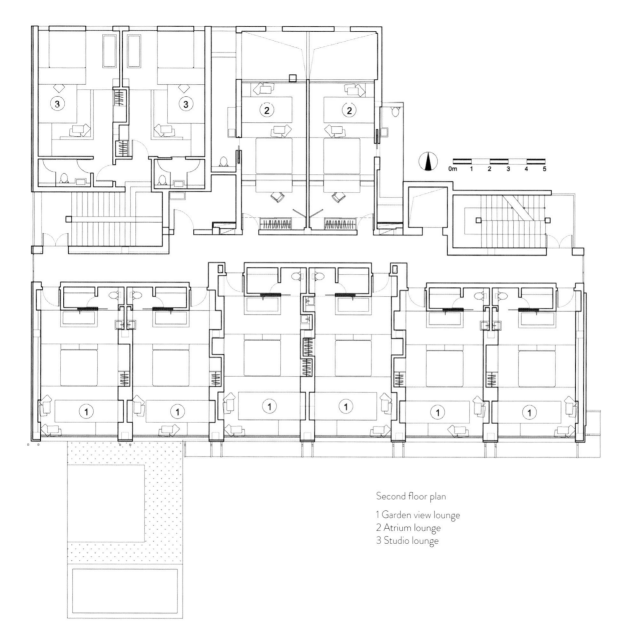

Second floor plan

1 Garden view lounge
2 Atrium lounge
3 Studio lounge

0m 1 2 3 4 5

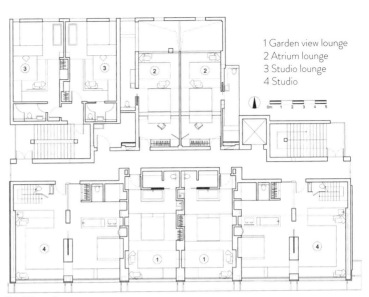

1 Garden view lounge
2 Atrium lounge
3 Studio lounge
4 Studio

Third floor plan

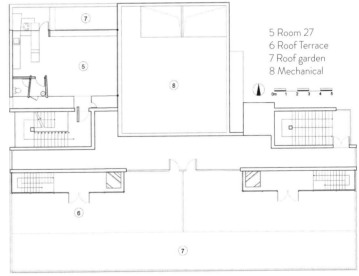

5 Room 27
6 Roof Terrace
7 Roof garden
8 Mechanical

Fourth floor plan

# Dream Hotel & Hostel

Studio Puisto Architects
Tampere, Finland
Photos: © Patrik Rastenberger, Marc Goodwin

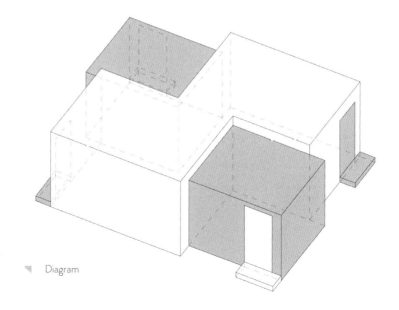

Diagram

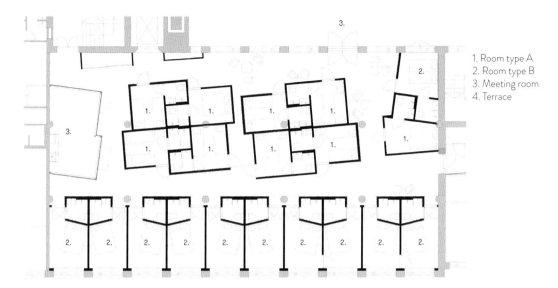

1. Room type A
2. Room type B
3. Meeting room
4. Terrace

Floor plan 1

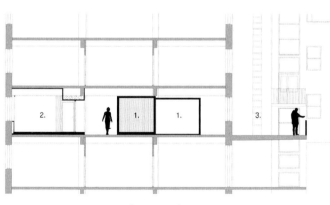

Section

1. Room type A
2. Room type B
3. Terrace

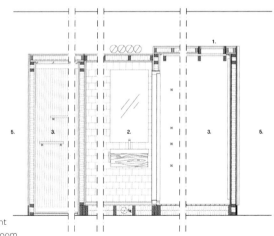

1. Skylight
2. Bathroom
3. Room
4. Technical floor
5. Public space

# Condesa Hotel

JSª / Javier Sánchez + India Mahdavi
Colonia Condesa, Mexico
Photos: © Luis Gordoa

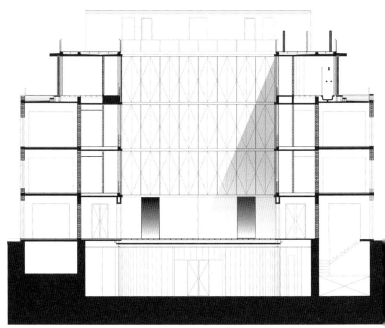

Cross section

0                                                    m

Access plan

0      m5

Rooms plan

0      m5

Roof plan

0      m5

# Flora House

VaSLab Architects
Phangnga, Thailand
Photos: © Jason Michael Lang

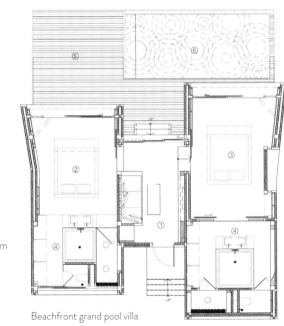

1 Living room
2 Bedroom
3 Master room
4 Bathroom
5 Decks
6 Pool

Beachfront grand pool villa

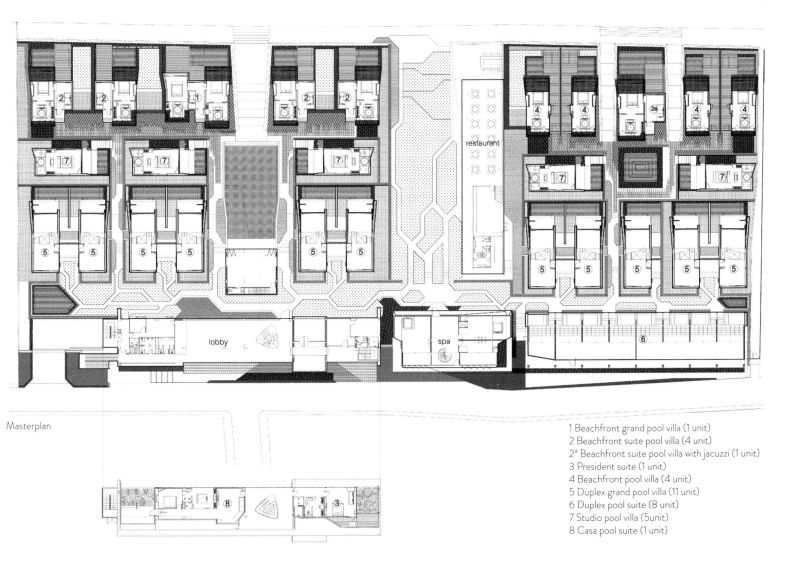

Masterplan

1 Beachfront grand pool villa (1 unit)
2 Beachfront suite pool villa (4 unit)
2ª Beachfront suite pool villa with jacuzzi (1 unit)
3 President suite (1 unit)
4 Beachfront pool villa (4 unit)
5 Duplex grand pool villa (11 unit)
6 Duplex pool suite (8 unit)
7 Studio pool villa (5unit)
8 Casa pool suite (1 unit)

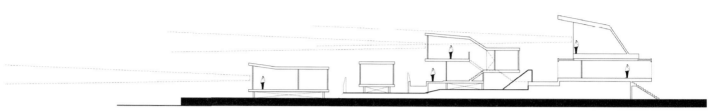

Section

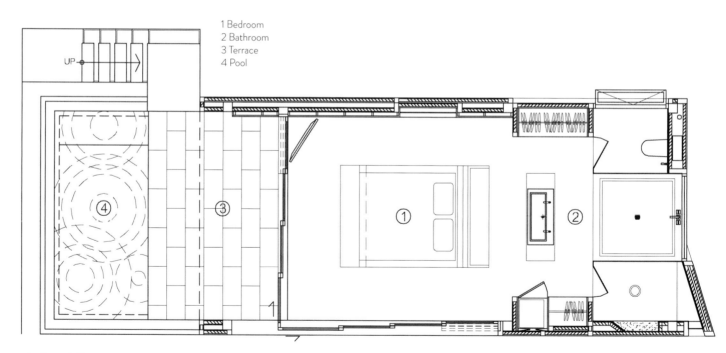

1 Bedroom
2 Bathroom
3 Terrace
4 Pool

UP

① Bedroom
② Bathroom
③ Terrace
④ Pool

Studio pool villa

# Generator Paris

Ory Associates
Paris, France
Photos: © Nikolas Koenig, Sinue Serra,
Valentine Tchoukhonine (rooftop)

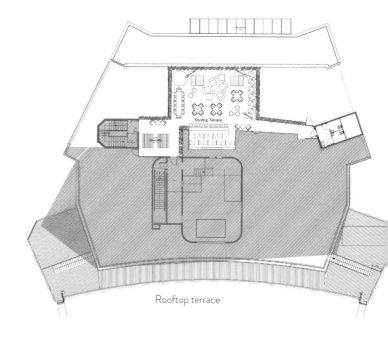

Rooftop terrace

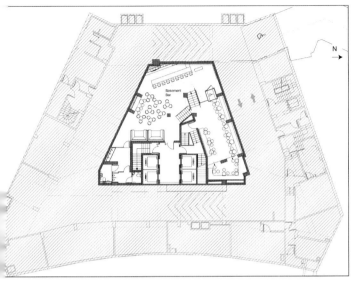

Lower level

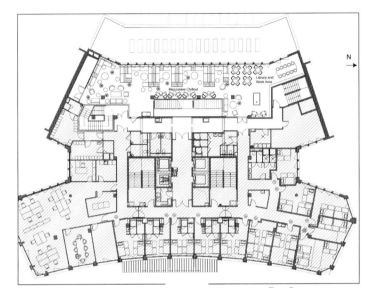

First floor

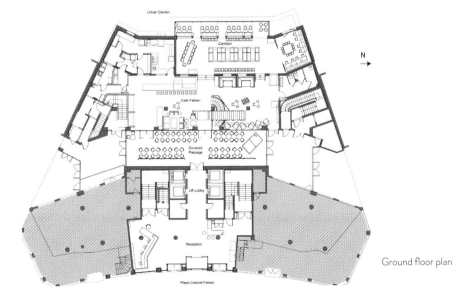

Ground floor plan

# Caldor Self Check in Hotel

Thomas Bärtl, Michael Prodinger, Guido Trampitsch
Vienna, Austria
Photos: © Severin Wurnig

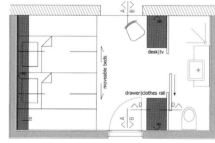

Floor plan double room

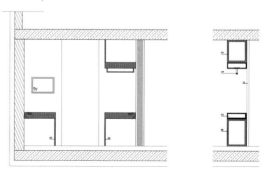

Section B-B                    Section D-D

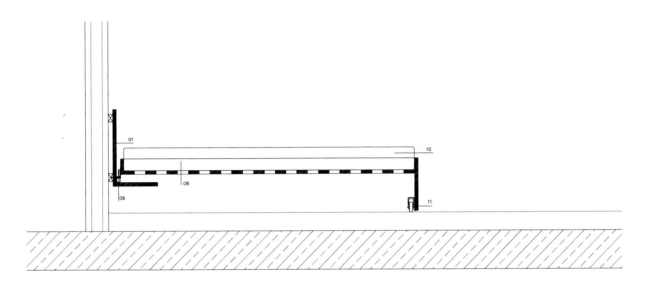

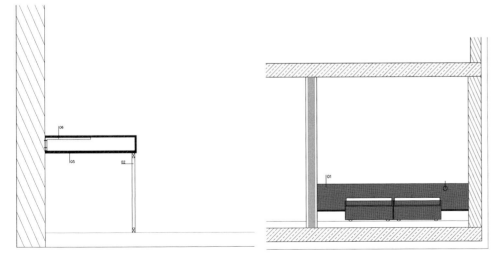

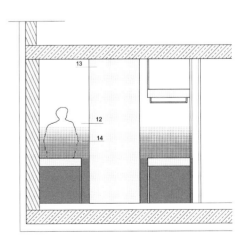

Tipical room: Details, plan and section

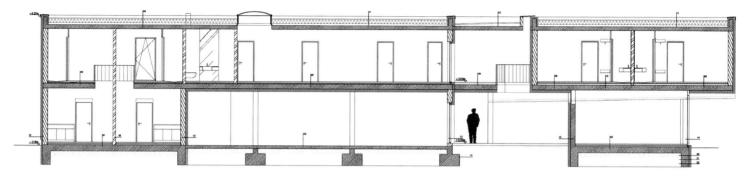

A-A Section

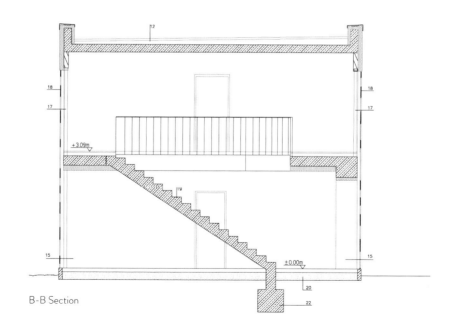

+3.09m

+0.00m

20

22

B-B Section

Elevation

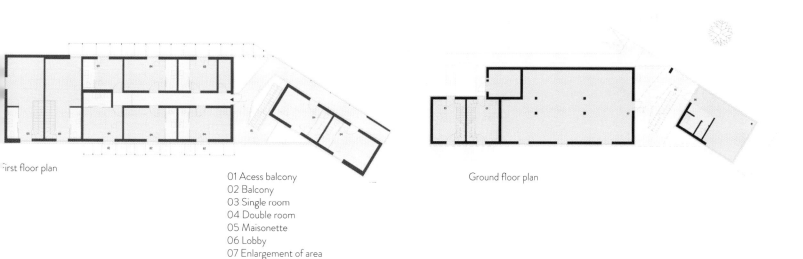

First floor plan

Ground floor plan

01 Acess balcony
02 Balcony
03 Single room
04 Double room
05 Maisonette
06 Lobby
07 Enlargement of area

# Consolación Hotel

Camprubí & Santacana Architects
Monroyo, Spain
Photos: © Jaime Font, Antonio Navarro & Pedro A. Pérez

Site plan

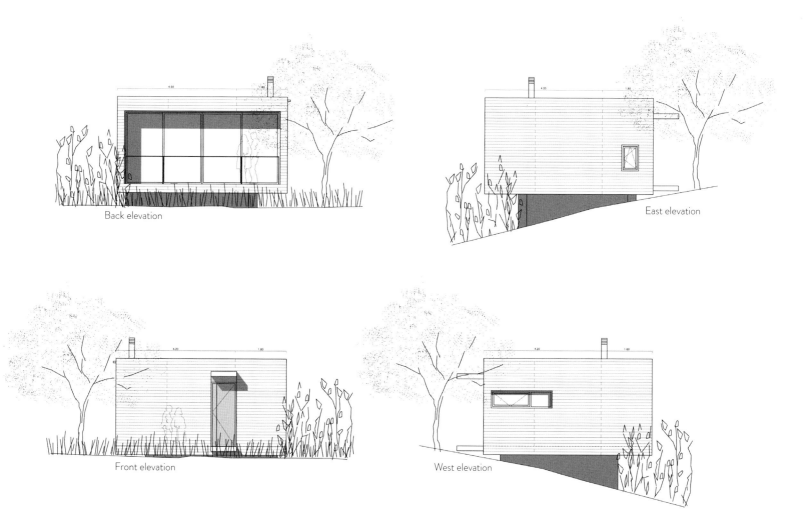

Back elevation

East elevation

Front elevation

West elevation

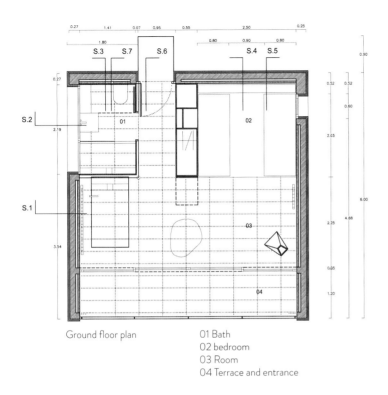

Ground floor plan

01 Bath
02 bedroom
03 Room
04 Terrace and entrance

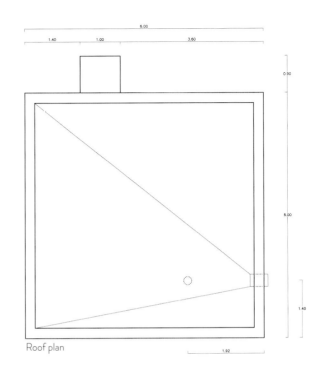

Roof plan

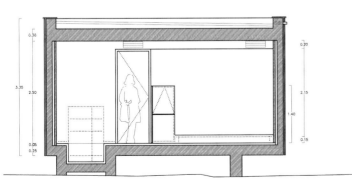

Section 1

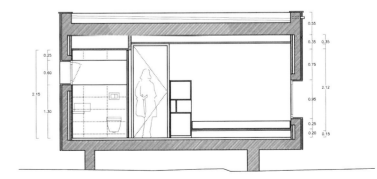

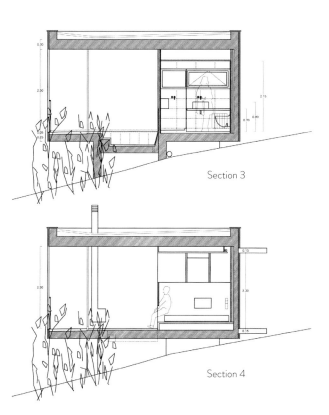

Section 5

Section 3

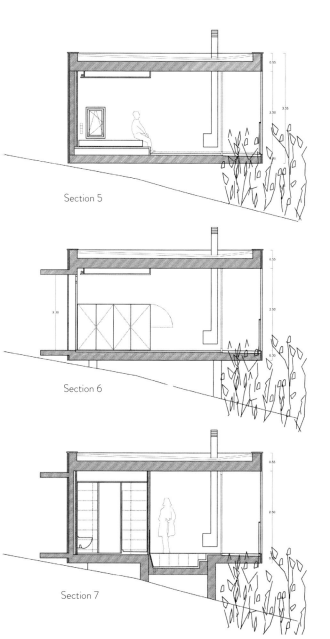

Section 6

Section 4

Section 7

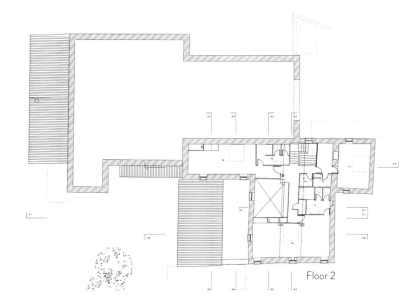

Floor 2

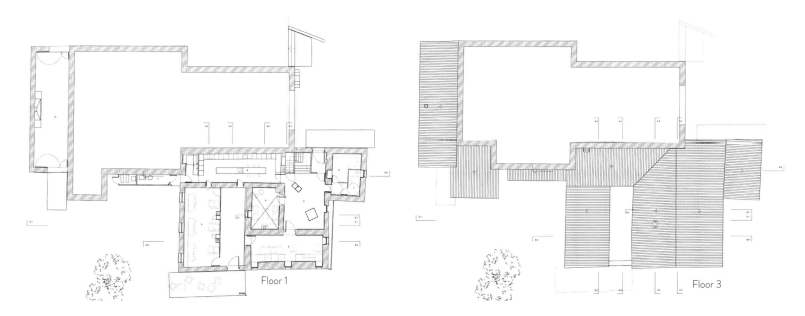

Floor 1

Floor 3

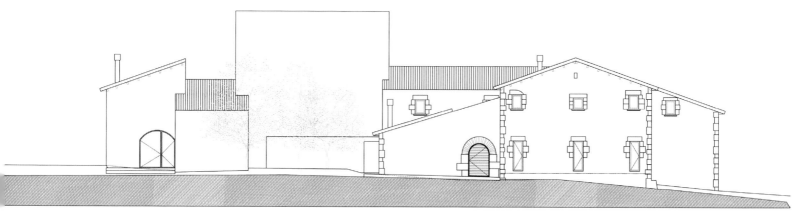

hwest elevation

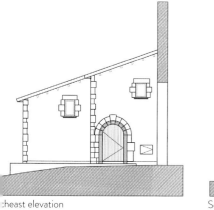

theast elevation

Southeast elevation

Northwest elevation

# Dream Downtown Hotel

Frank Fusaro, Handel Architects
New York, USA
Photos: © Bruce Damonte, Philip Ennis

Second floor plan

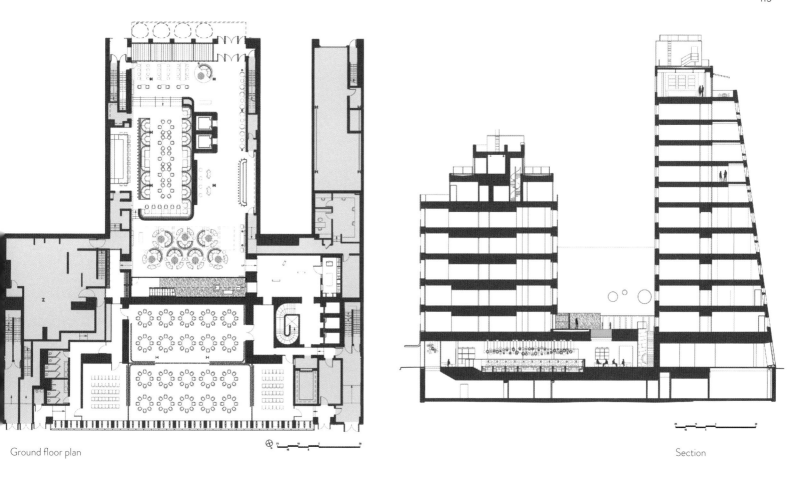

Ground floor plan

Section

# Hostalet

Toni Gironés Architects
Cadaqués, Spain
Photos: © Estudi d'arquitectura Toni Gironés

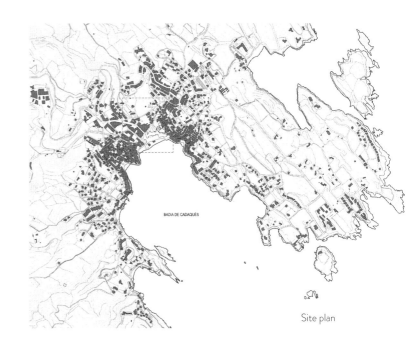

Site plan

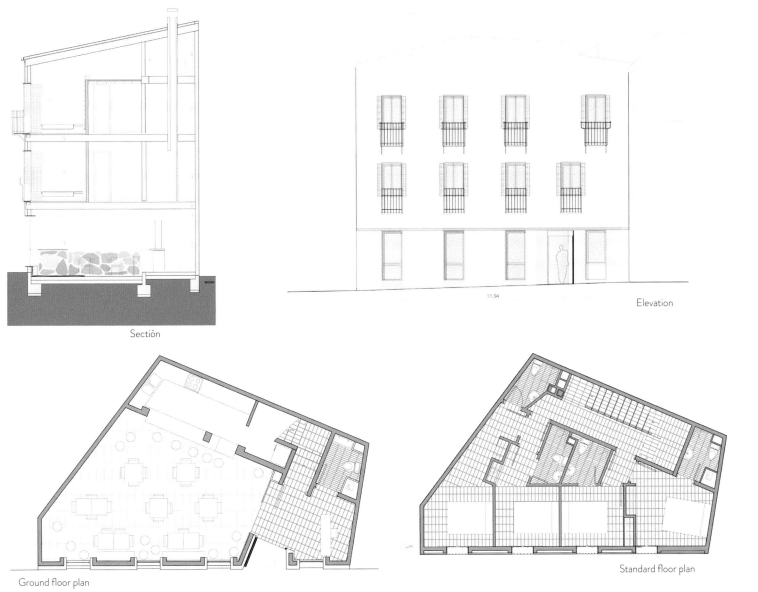

Sectión

Elevation

11.94

Ground floor plan

Standard floor plan

# Lone Hotel

3LHD Architects
Rovinj, Croatia
Photos: © Cat Vinton, Damir Fabijani´c, 3LHD Archive

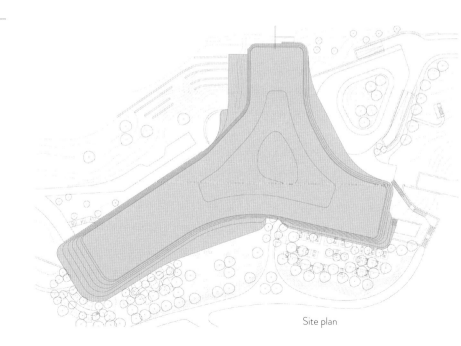

Site plan

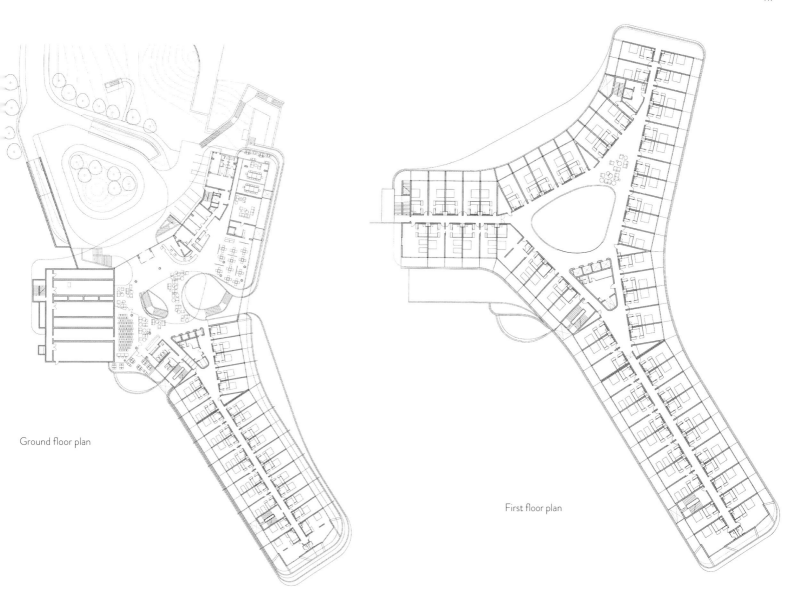

Ground floor plan

First floor plan

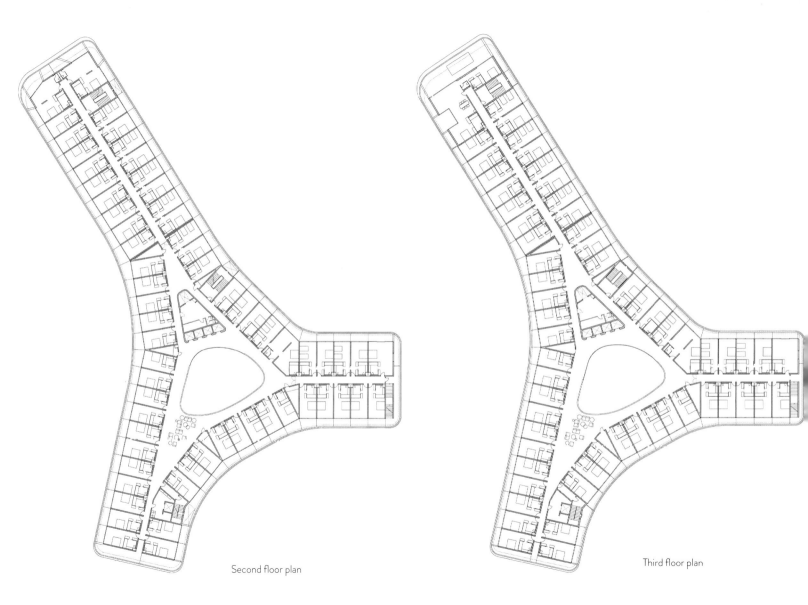

Second floor plan

Third floor plan

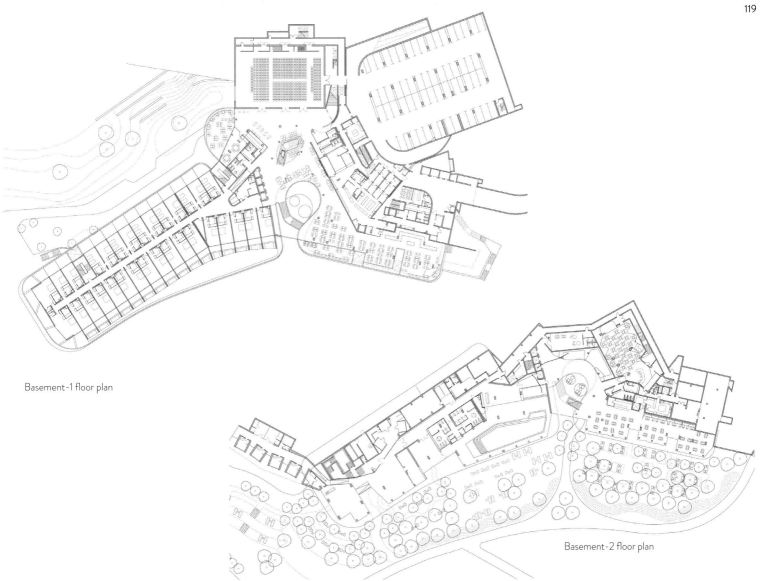

Basement-1 floor plan

Basement-2 floor plan

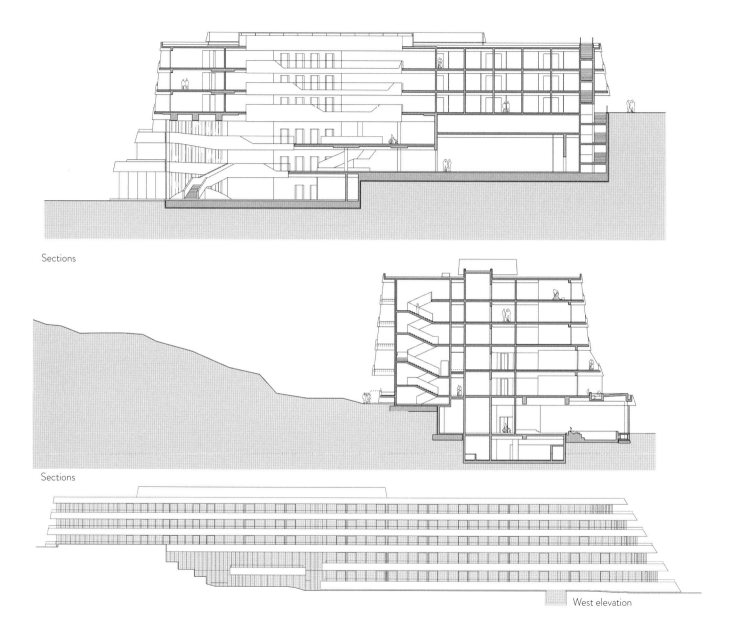

Sections

Sections

West elevation

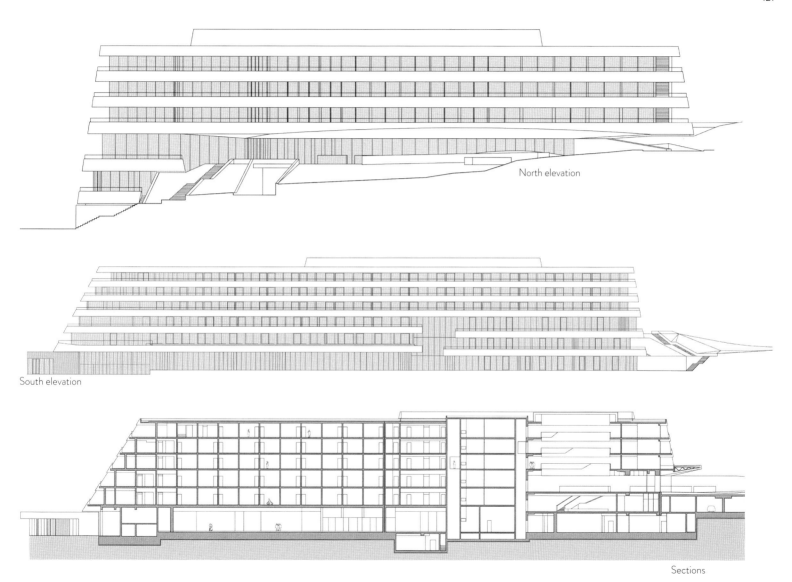

North elevation

South elevation

Sections

# Wellness Sotelia Hotel

Enota
Podčetrtek, Slovenia
Photos: © Miran Kambič

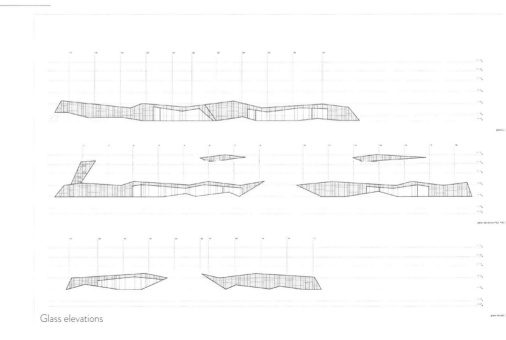

Glass elevations

Ground floor plan

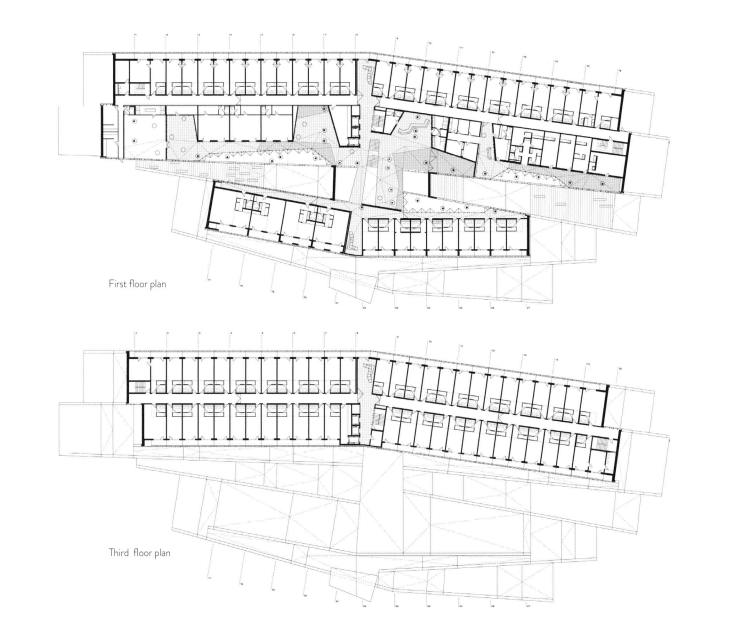

First floor plan

Third floor plan

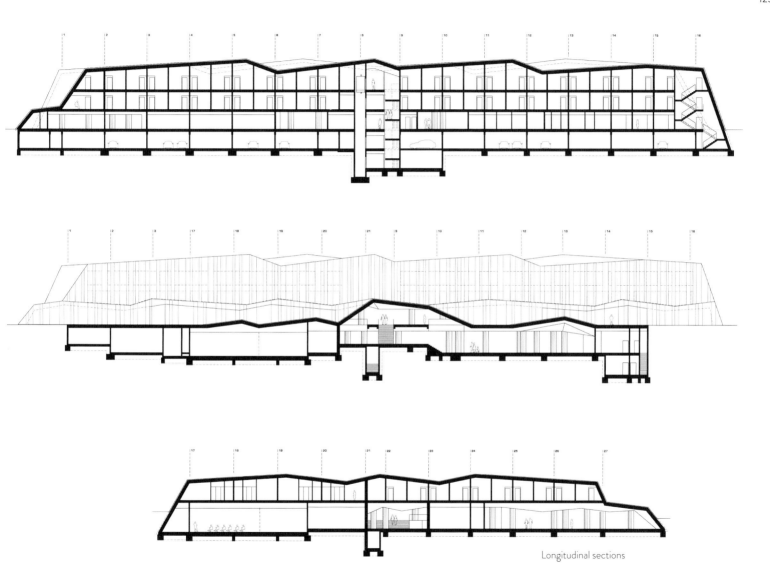

Longitudinal sections

# Nowhere But Sajima

Yasutaka Yoshimura Architects
Kanagawa, Japan
Photos: © Chiaki Yasukawa, Yasutaka Yoshimura

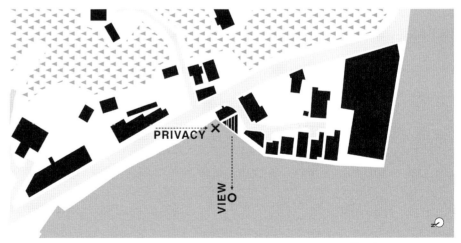

Site plan

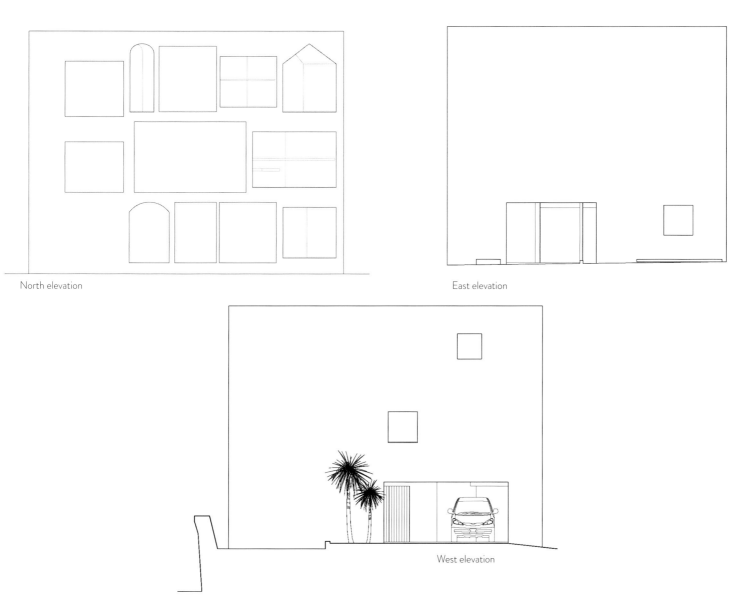

North elevation

East elevation

West elevation

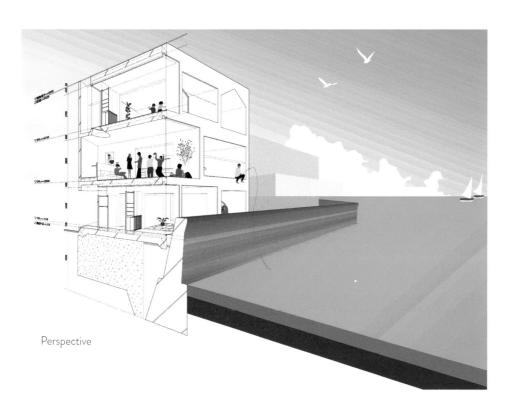

Perspective

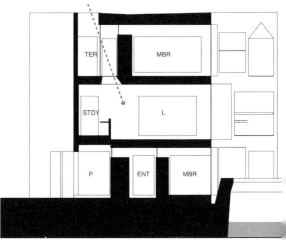

Sections

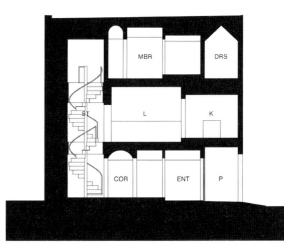

Sections

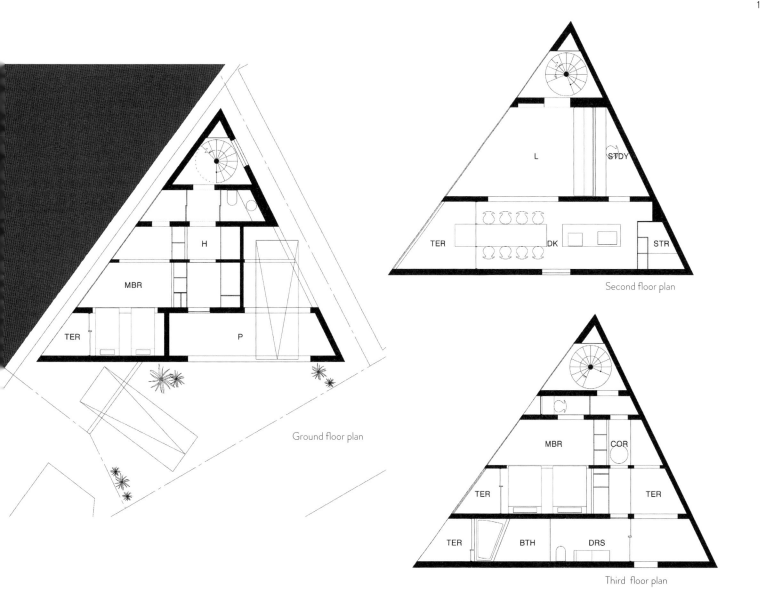

Ground floor plan

Second floor plan

Third floor plan

# Boutique Palafito 1326 Hotel

Edward Rojas Architects
Castro, Chiloé, Chile
Photos: © Carlos Mallagaray, María José Lira,
Andrés Salinero & Edward Rojas

Site plan

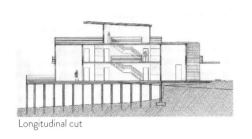

Longitudinal cut

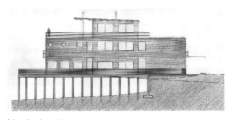

North elevation

West elevation

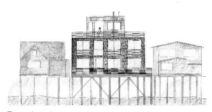

East elevation

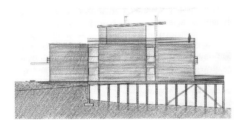

South elevation

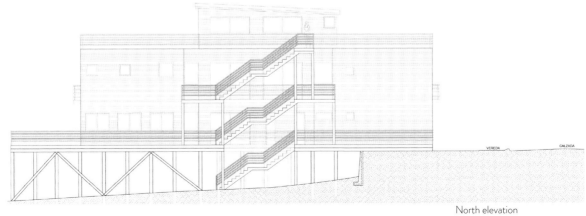

North elevation

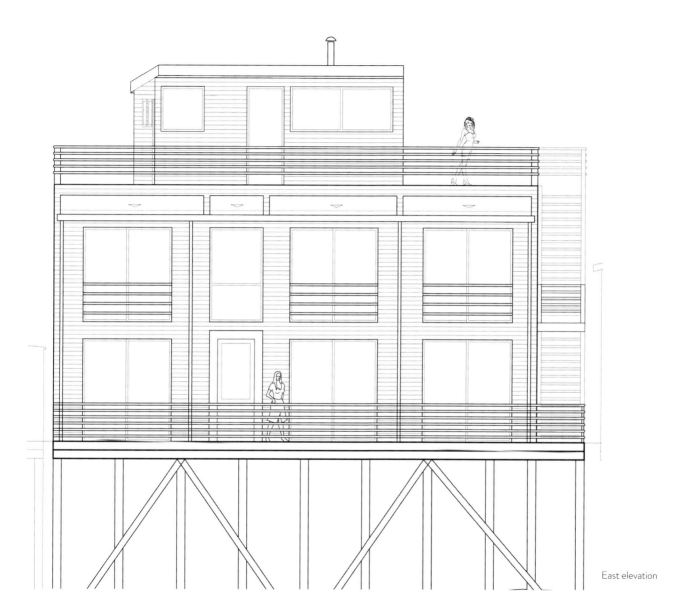

East elevation

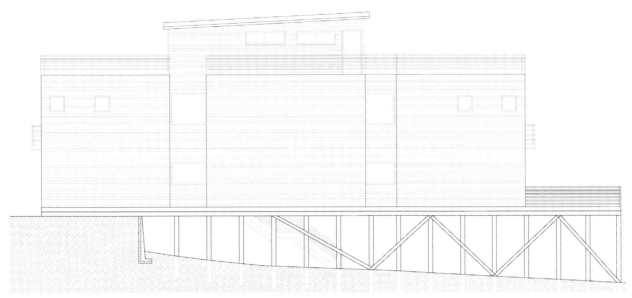

South elevation

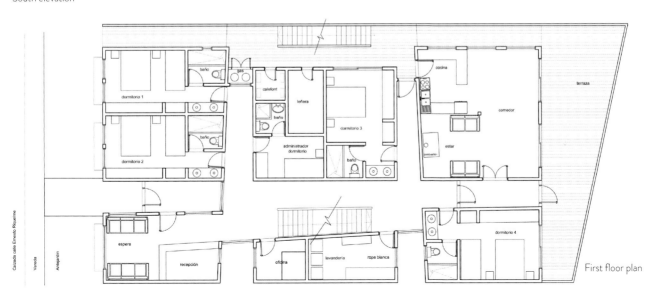

First floor plan

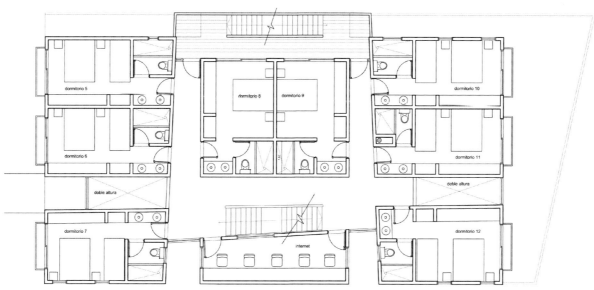

Second floor plan

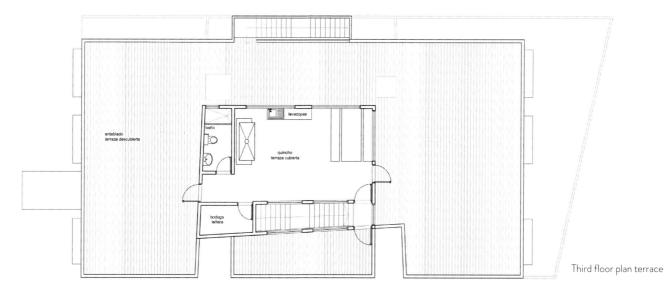

Third floor plan terrace

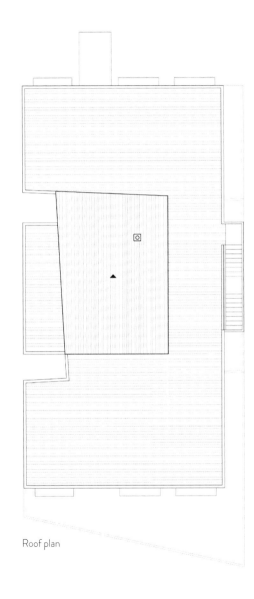

Roof plan

# Generator Hamburg

Coido Architects
Hamburg, Germany
Photos: © Nikolas Koenig, Sinue Serra

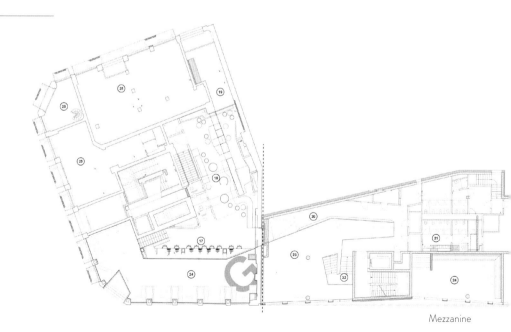

Mezzanine

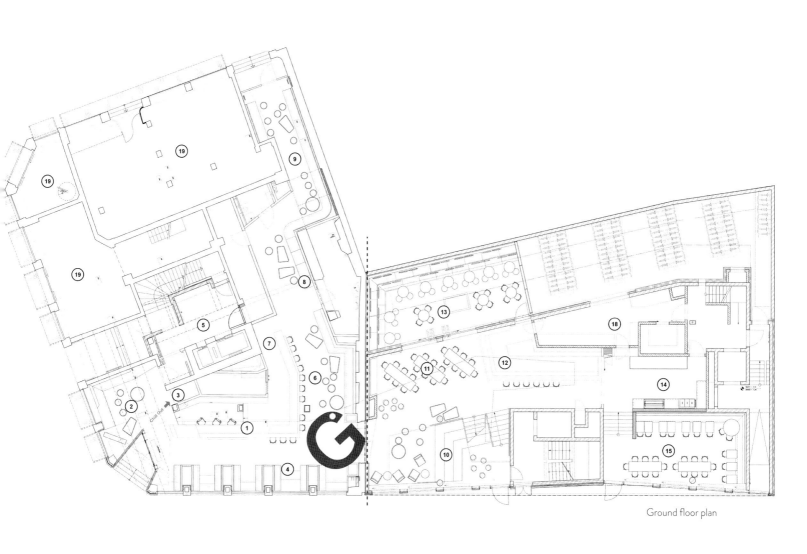

Ground floor plan

Second floor plan

Third floor plan

# Piece Hostel Sanjo

OH Architecture
Kyoto, Japan
Photos: © Satoshi Shigeta, Toshiyuki Yano

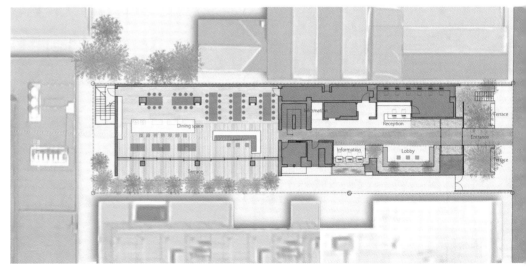

Ground floor plan

Second and third floor plan

Fourth floor plan

Fifth floor plan

First floor plan

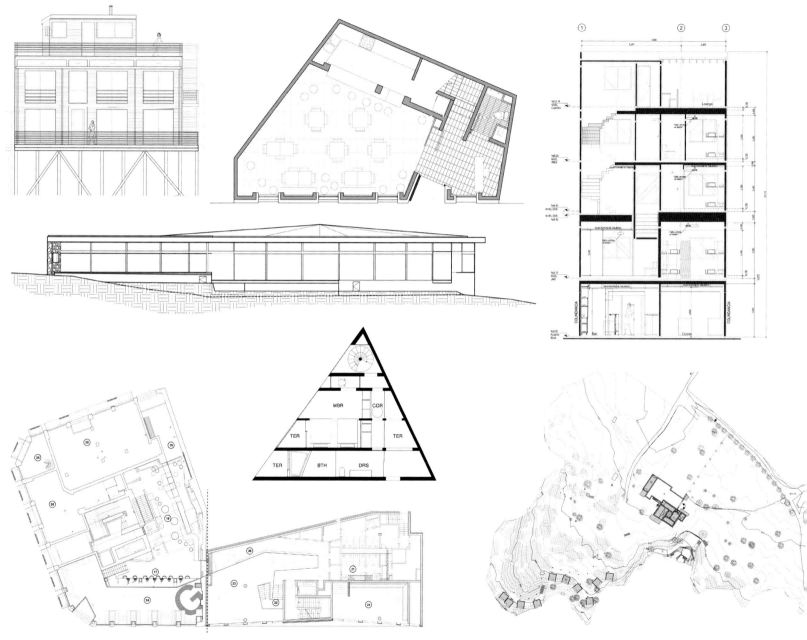